CALL IT

BY

ELLEN METZ

Call It
Copyright © 2018 by Ellen Metz

ISBN (Print Edition): 978-1-54392-649-1
ISBN (eBook Edition): 978-1-54392-650-7

TABLE OF CONTENTS

The Emergency Department

———•◆•———

1990

My coworker and I shoved a red metal cabinet on wheels from the hallway into a treatment room next to an empty stretcher. It looked like an ordinary tool cart you might see in an automotive garage. I quickly twisted off a small disposable lock, so we could open the drawers and pull out prefilled syringes of emergency drugs. I stabbed a bag of intravenous fluid with some plastic tubing, and then primed the tubing with the fluid so it was ready to be attached to the patient. My coworker pulled out the syringes of the drugs used for resuscitation. Then we both put on paper gowns and latex gloves and waited for the emergency squad. They were on the way with a three-year-old boy, found unresponsive and floating in his parents' backyard pool. We tried to control our adrenaline, but no matter how many times we had been through this, a life-and-death call from the EMS (emergency medical services) still felt like an electric prod applied directly to our nervous systems.

The paramedics were performing CPR as they rushed through the door. I looked at the tiny body and knew the situation was probably hopeless. The boy's color was bluish-grey, his limbs were flaccid, and *Oh God*, I suddenly realized, *he's the same size and age as my son.*

The ER doctor and other nurses joined us at the bedside. Someone cut off the boy's clothes as one of my teammates hooked him up to the cardiac monitor. All motion paused momentarily while everyone looked at the monitor's screen. He was a straight line—his heart was not beating.

"Continue CPR," the ER doctor said. He turned and asked the squad paramedics for the time of the boy's last dose of epinephrine. "Repeat the epinephrine, give me the ET tube!" he shouted.

The ER nurses relieved the paramedics and continued performing CPR, then the doctor inserted the ET tube, a plastic tube that is inserted down the throat for better oxygen delivery. We gave the boy multiple doses of intravenous medications in addition to the oxygen. As each medication was given I recorded the time. The boy's heart did not respond, and we all knew the outcome was inevitable.

The ER doctor finally said, "Call it," and one of the nurses looked at the clock on the wall.

"Time of death, five-fifteen P.M.," the nurse said. And so it was recorded.

A sense of devastation loomed in the air because the victim was a child. Then everyone except me left the room to return to the other patients. I had charting to complete, and then I would make the call to the coroner.

Whenever we resuscitate a patient, one nurse is designated to follow up with the family and complete the paperwork. We take turns performing this duty; that evening, it was my turn. I gagged back my tears and wiped the boy's face with a washcloth then smoothed his hair down, attempting to make him more presentable for his family. I bagged up the remnants of his clothes, including a tiny pair of underpants that were stained from an opened sphincter he had when he gave up his life.

The parents were in the quiet room that was used for life-altering conversations. I had been present at many of these conversations but had not dealt with the death of a child since I had become a mother. The mother was talking with another nurse when the doctor and I entered. Her conversation was nonsensical; she wasn't ready to acknowledge what had happened, and her mind had clearly left the current time and place. The father filled in some pieces, he said his wife had spotted the child floating in their above ground pool from an upstairs window. His older brothers had apparently left the ladder on the pool; they were just school-age kids. It was all an accident.

The father asked to see his son, and I took him to the room. He looked, and then he backed up to the wall for support. I didn't have much to offer other than my presence and a hand. I have no idea how long we stood there before we returned to the quiet room. As was customary, I asked the parents if they wanted to call a minister and if they wanted the name of a funeral home. In less than an hour, the child was picked up and the parents had returned to their home.

While restocking the red metal cart, I saw our ER doctor in his office, sitting at his desk and staring into space. I stopped what I was doing, walked into his office, and sat down in the chair across from him. We shook our heads in sadness. I didn't know him well, but I knew he had a young child at home. Miraculously, I was still able to control my tears.

When I arrived home after midnight I changed my clothes. Only then did I sit and allow myself to cry. I poured myself some whiskey, downed it, and then continued crying so hard that I retched. I woke my husband and told him what had happened. He listened, patted my arm, and fell back asleep. He couldn't comprehend the events in the ER because he hadn't been there cleaning that little body. I didn't fall asleep until the early hours of the morning.

The tears started again the next morning as I dressed my son and made breakfast. Sadness was perceptible that evening among the returning nursing staff. We all wondered how the mother was doing. We could all relate.

When the weekend arrived, I went alone to the lake near our home. The sight and sound of the water on the rocks were soothing, but I knew it would take some time to get over this. The instructors in nursing school had never taught us how to deal with tragedy.

A few months later, a "thank you" note arrived from the child's mother. She talked about acceptance and her belief in a higher power.

CHAPTER ONE

Nursing School

September 1969

My parents and I entered a brick building that had been built circa 1900. We saw a small sitting room on the left and a wooden counter on the right. A shelf with cubby holes was mounted on the wall behind the counter. The entire room looked like it could have been the registration area at an old hotel. An elderly woman behind the desk greeted us then sent us down the hall toward a reception room.

The room was large, with a collection of dated and mismatched furniture arranged on a wood floor. Waist-high bookcases lined two of the walls. The center of the room was anchored by a rug and had a television, a couch and a couple of chairs. A ping-pong table, sat in a back corner. Smiling women at fold-up tables waved us over. They introduced themselves as students and instructors and handed me a class schedule, several information packets and my room keys.

I had no frame of reference about nursing on that day, other than some sketchy memories of a book series I had read in middle school. The series featured a nurse named Cherry Ames, who solved mysteries like Nancy Drew. I decided to become a nurse after a chance encounter with a high school friend's older sister. She was in nursing school, and, one day, while I was visiting my friend, her sister had come home wearing her student uniform. She dropped a starched white nurse's cap and a pile of medical books on the kitchen table. She looked *important*.

The school I selected was in the city and offered a three-year training program to become a registered nurse. It was associated with a hospital less than a half block up the street. The original hospital, which was now mostly empty, and a separate building used for mental health services stood directly across the street from the school. The rest of the street was a collection of run-down clapboard homes shaded by overgrown trees. Most registered nurses graduated from schools like this, until the 1980s, when the number of colleges and universities offering associate and baccalaureate nursing degrees increased. Hospitals supported these nursing programs because they were a good source of recruits.

There were three floors of dorm rooms above the classrooms, which sat at ground level. My room was in a newer extension that had been added to the original building where we had entered. The room had a large window on the back wall that provided good natural light. The furniture was painted metal and appeared relatively new. My roommate had apparently already arrived, but she was not physically present. Instead, we were greeted by a molded Styrofoam head covered with a blonde wig and a football poster sitting on one of two desks. I placed a flowerpot with fabric flowers on the empty desk. Beside the flowerpot, I set down a bulletin board. Both were gifts from my mom. She was a *Woman's Day Magazine* aficionado, and these were featured crafts.

I unpacked some clothes, and then we were ready to explore.

Each floor had a small kitchen and lounge area with a TV. There were communal bathrooms on opposite ends of the floor. I immediately noticed a single phone booth in the hall then realized there was no phone in my dorm room. I would soon learn the rules for the phone. Whenever the phone rang, the person closest to the phone booth answered it then hollered out the name of the person requested by the caller. Anyone using the phone was expected to be reasonably brief. (Today, it's hard to believe today that a single phone booth was sufficient for an entire floor of young women. At the time, a personal electronic device was a radio!)After the parents left, all students new and old met in the gym for cookies, punch, and corny songs about nursing. The senior students then offered a tour of the school.

We started in the basement of the original building. The area was named the Ratskeller and it had mildew-scented wicker furniture. An alcove off to one side housed our mailboxes and a few vending machines. A hallway off the other side of the room led to a tunnel, which connected the school to the basement of the hospital. The tunnel looked like a subway without the train and was a pleasant surprise. We would never need coats or umbrellas when we walked from the school to the hospital.

The seniors told us we could entertain our boyfriends in the reception room or in the basement. No males were ever allowed in the dorm quarters, and our conduct—and virtue—would be monitored by the staff of housemothers. We had a curfew, and all of us had to sign in and out on a clipboard at the front door desk. Whenever a guest would arrive at the front desk, the housemother would page us overhead with the words, "Miss Jones—" or Miss *Whoever* "—you have a visitor at the desk."

The tour continued to the senior quarters, which were on the upper floors of the old building. We could take the stairs or an old elevator that had a glass door and a gate. The elevator chugged, so I chose the stairs.

The original dorm rooms were spacious, with high ceilings. Transoms ran above all the doors. The wooden windows appeared to be original but some were apparently not fully functional since I noticed rulers and even books were used to prop them open. There were single and double rooms. All were furnished with antique beds, dressers and chairs. The majority of the furniture was made from oak but there were some beautiful carved cherry and walnut pieces with marble tops. The furniture would become chic collectibles in the years to come, but in 1969 they had not yet been discovered. The toilet and shower surrounds were made with real marble. Despite the larger rooms and some charming furniture, the senior dorm had one big downside. No air-conditioning. It was September when I arrived, and the rooms were still uncomfortably hot, even though fans whirled throughout the dorm. I was happy to be living in the newer extension, with air-conditioning.

As my first semester progressed, I didn't see much of my roommate, because we were on different schedules. Half of my class sat in the classroom on Mondays and Tuesdays then attended clinical practice in the hospital on Thursdays and Fridays. The schedule was reversed for the other group. Obviously, students became friendly and bonded with other students who were on their schedule. Wednesdays were half days, and we all attended class together. A professor from a local community college came to the nursing school to teach psychology and sociology classes. The hospital chaplain, a Catholic priest, taught classes on medical ethics.

When the weather cooled, and we opened our windows, I awakened to the smell of bread; a commercial bakery was only a few blocks away—what a pleasure! On the days we had classes we would put on our lab coats and walk through the tunnel to the hospital's cafeteria for breakfast. We had been required to purchase a uniform and a lab coat before we started classes; the lab coat was a godsend. The coat's thread count was high enough so we could wear it over just our underwear or our pajamas. No one could tell. Additionally, we felt official and important whenever we wore them. We had a strict dress code for our clinical days in the hospital. It included a light blue uniform dress, white stockings and white tie shoes (familiarly called "clinics"), and a white starched nursing cap bobby pinned to our hair. Long hair could not be worn loose; it had to be tied back or pinned in a bun under our caps. Fingernails had to be trimmed, and jewelry was not permitted, other than a watch and a wedding ring.

Student caps were plain. After graduation we would add a brown velvet ribbon to the cuff on our caps. All nursing schools had distinctive caps. I noticed different caps throughout the hospital. One reminded me of the paper frill on a holiday pork crown roast. Others looked like a witch's hats. Some looked like bird wings. Regardless of their impracticality, caps served to identify nurses; they were also a status symbol.

Our instructors were registered nurses—except for the science teacher, the hospital chaplain, and a few professors who were under contract from the community college. One of our first classes was devoted to how to address and talk with patients; a big emphasis of the class was on courtesy. Calling a patient by their first name without their permission was taboo.

We were told to offer our seats at the nurse's station to the doctors, if necessary. Our biggest challenge would be learning the medical lingo, because a significant amount of it was derived from Latin. We had to memorize a long and maddening list of words and abbreviations associated with medical treatments and the administration of medications. For example, *ac* means take before meals, *prn* means take as needed, *qd* means daily; *os* means left eye, *cholecystectomy* means removal of a gallbladder.

We learned how to take patients' vital signs, which include temperature, pulse, blood pressure, and respiration rate, and then we progressed to learning how to give bed baths. Bathing patients was still a part of a nurse's job in those days, though it wouldn't be in the years ahead. Somehow, our instructors failed to make clear that two pans were in each patient's bedside stand—a bedpan and a bath pan. So, during our clinical practice, when we were assigned to a patient in the hospital, one of my classmates filled up the bed-pan to bathe her patient but stopped when she thought it just didn't look right. She had the good sense to look to see what everyone else was using to bathe their patients. We all had a good laugh.

Our clinical practice days started and ended with a group conference, and we were expected to come prepared. We each visited the hospital the evening before the conference to introduce ourselves to our assigned patient and review his or her chart. We looked up the patient's condition and detailed it on an index card. We would be asked to discuss the doctor's diagnosis and any abnormal signs and symptoms the patient presented that would alert us to contact the doctor. The objective was to help us to develop our critical thinking skills. After all, the doctor would be seeing the patient only a few minutes a day but the nurses would be assessing the patient over the course of an eight-hour shift. We were going to be the doctor's eyes and ears. Patients could always refuse being cared for by a student...but I never heard of one who did.

Dorm life was fun, and we developed our friendships by playing cards in the lounge after class. Double-deck pinochle was the game of choice. I learned the game from my new friends from the farm communities. They all seemed to be accomplished card players. As the cards were dealt and we played our tricks, the room grew smoky from menthol cigarettes. Many of the student nurses smoked then. Doctors smoked too even in the nurse's station. Visitors smoked in the cafeteria. Patients smoked in their rooms. Cigarette commercials featuring beautiful people by refreshing, inviting waterfalls played on TV. The health issues associated with cigarettes had not yet been widely publicized, and cigarettes were cheap.

After cards we sometimes had a potluck supper. Our shared food might be tuna, soup, or chips, but there was one item the city girls had trouble with: milk in jars. The city girls wouldn't touch it, because milk *had* to come in a carton stating it had been pasteurized. But some of the farm girls would bring fresh milk, straight from the cows, in jars that had been filled back on their farms. Apparently, the fresh milk was fine, because I can't recall any of the farm girls coming down with any gastrointestinal illnesses; but personally, I never took the leap of faith required to drink it.

A TV show called *Medical Center* was on the air during this time. We all had a crush on Chad Everett, the television star who played Dr. Joe Gannon. We sat on the floor and on the little vinyl couches that had been arranged around the TV in our lounge, and we tried to diagnose the illness that was ailing the featured patient. We shouted our guesses and applauded ourselves when we were right. I'm pretty sure we all thought about finding someone in our lives like Joe.

In anatomy lab we sat on stools at long tables with slate tops. The lab was much like a high school chemistry lab, only larger. The focal point of the first year was dissecting a cat...or at least that is what I remember the most, anyway. Each student was given a cat cadaver and our assignment for the next several weeks was to identify and flag specific muscles, tendons, and organs. The cats were kept in plastic bags in rubber trash cans. It was a very disagreeable sight—cats with rigor mortis—but I remember the smell of them over and above all else. The smell was formaldehyde, and it was then I learned to breathe through my mouth. This breathing technique would serve me well over the course of my career.

Microbiology was difficult. Try to process and pronounce words like *enterobacter aerogenes, staphylococcus,* or *klebsiella,* which are commonly known as bacteria or germs in a layperson's terms. We learned about helpful bacteria, which can be found in our bowels and which aid in digestion, but our major focus was bacteria that cause disease.

If a patient under our care developed an infection, it was important to determine the type of bacteria causing the infection, so the correct antibiotic could be ordered. We went through the process in our microbiology lab in much the same way it is done in the hospital. Every student was given a vial of liquid called their "unknown." The liquid in the vial contained bacteria, and we had to determine the identity of the bacteria by testing it with various reagents and by placing some of it on a round plastic dish (called a petri dish) with a jellylike substance. Every species of bacterium exhibits a unique color and growth pattern when plated and tested with reagents.The procedure for identifying bacteria is well established; but first-year students sometimes contaminate reagents, and that sort of confuses the results. I recall expending a great deal of time and energy trying to identify my unknown. My tests with various reagents did not yield a definitive color, and the bacteria in the sample on my plate showed very little growth. I made my best guess as to the identity of the unknown; fortunately, I was right. I was relieved...and ready to move along. Microbiology was my most challenging class.

When we started pharmacology class, the first thing we were told was: *All medication is a potential poison.* I have never forgotten that statement. It remains true today for all prescription and over-the-counter medications: people are allergic to certain drugs. Drugs can interact adversely with each other. Patients take their medications incorrectly. The pharmacology book was our largest and heaviest textbook. I can't fathom what the size of a complete hard copy book must be like today, given the explosion of new categories of drugs: Cholesterol-lowering drugs, psychiatric medications to elevate mood, and stomach acid blockers are a few of the categories of medications that have been developed since I was in training. It's hard to believe that patients with ulcers were once treated every few hours with an ounce of cream mixed with an ounce of Maalox. We kept both products at the patient's bedside stand; the carton of cream sat in a bowl of ice. Studies later showed that this regimen was detrimental.

We practiced preparing and administering medications in the classroom before being allowed to administer any drugs to our patients. When we visited the hospital the night before our clinical day, we recorded all of our patients' medications on separate index cards (in addition to the diagnosis card). When we returned to the dorm we looked up the category of each drug, the reasons for the drug's use, and the drug's potential side effects. The next day, our instructor would check our cards as we prepared the medications. The preparation area was in a mini kitchen on each unit in the hospital. Every patient had a small plastic medication box labeled with his or her room number. We poured the pills into tiny paper cups under the watchful eye of the instructor. If a patient was to receive medication as a shot, we prepared syringes and placed them with the pill cups on a small plastic tray we would take into the patient's room. We asked the patient his or her name and checked their armband, even if we knew them and had been in their room all morning.

Giving a shot marked a major milestone. The abbreviation used for administering a medication by a "shot" (also called an injection) is *IM*, which means "intramuscular." When administering a shot, the nurse chooses where to place the injection: in the arm, in the leg, or in the buttock. The amount and viscosity (thickness) of the medication determines the choice of injection site. I clearly remember my first IM. It was a pain medication for a postoperative patient. I was scared, and my hands were shaking. However, my instructor was kind and calm, so the injection went smoothly. It also helped that she pulled the plunger of the syringe back for me—a maneuver we performed to make sure the syringe's needle was not in the patient's blood vessel before we injected the medication.

Today, with a few exceptions, such as immunizations, flu shots, or perhaps a vitamin preparation like B_{12}, medications are not commonly given intramuscularly today. I have been told that absorption of intramuscular medications can be somewhat unpredictable, and that is why this administration method has fallen out of favor. Instead, most pain medications are currently given intravenously or by mouth. The same is true for antibiotics, which nurses administer either intravenously or orally. One day I was helping change the bed of an elderly man who was bleeding from his bowels. He was a bilateral amputee who was confused and screaming profanities. The room was very hot, and the sight and smell totally nauseated me. This happens a lot to medical rookies: the feeling that you are going to faint. I made a quick exit to the nursing station, where I sat on the floor and brought my head down toward my knees. I thought I heard the ocean in my ears—a phenomenon I had read about in books but had never thought really happened. I did not pass out, but I realized that nurses are not immune to foul sights and smells. Over the years, many people have said to me, "I don't know how you do it." Well, we all succumb, at times. Many times, throughout my career, after a particularly messy cleanup, I heard vomiting through the bathroom door of the staff lounge—even from the head nurse. We try to breathe through our mouths to negate the "smell factor" and think about being somewhere else. Truthfully, though, messy cleanups are not an everyday occurrence.

After we had conquered the basics of working on the medical and surgical floors, we moved on to caring for "bones" on the orthopedic floor. When I first saw patients with their limbs swinging in hammocks, I was very intimidated. Traction looked complicated. But we learned how to deal with it and how to clean and assess the sites where pins had been inserted to keep the patients' bones in place until they healed. The most important thing about a cast is to make certain it doesn't compromise circulation. So, we frequently checked the color and the temperature of the body part hanging out of the cast, to make certain it was normal and similar in color and temperature to the limb on the other side without the cast.

Bathing patients who were in traction or who had a full leg or body cast was a challenge. The same was true if they needed to use a bedpan, or we needed to change the sheets on their bed. To make these tasks easier on the patient, a metal triangle was suspended from a pole over the top of the bed; we encouraged patients to grab the triangle, so they could help lift themselves up while we performed our tasks. However, sometimes the patient was too weak. We had to work as a team to move these patients. We considered ourselves very fortunate when there was a male orderly on the floor who could add some muscle to our task. I first understood the meaning of *tragedy* while rotating to the orthopedic floor. My assignment was a young male who was the victim of a car accident. When I reviewed his chart, I was horrified—he was my age, and he was essentially paralyzed from about the nipple line down. The accident had left him a quadriplegic. Then I recognized his name; he had dated one of my classmates when I was in high school, though he had attended a different school.

The patient's condition was so incredibly grim. *How do I talk about it with him?* I wondered. *How do I act with a positive disposition in the face of such a thing with no real hope of reversal? What do I say? How do I come up with a cheerful voice?* This was not covered in class. I manufactured a cheery mood and went into "task mode." I completed my shift without ever discussing anything specific about the patient's condition or his understanding of his long-term outlook. He was on what was called a circo-electric bed, which was state-of-the-art at the time. Two huge wheels held two stretchers that sandwiched the patient. Throughout the day, we used the wheels to rotate the patient from his back to his stomach;

the top stretcher was removed after the rotation. The bed and the rotation were designed to reduce the development of pressure sores. I remember washing his hair...and all I was thinking about was that he would need to be bathed and assisted with his eating and bowel functions the rest of his life. He would have a permanent drainage device for his urine, and he might never have a private life. I hoped that, eventually, his medical progress would give him a quality of life that he found somewhat acceptable. I knew rehabilitative hospitals taught patients to make the best of any faculties and body parts that still functioned. I could not wait for this day with my quadriplegic patient to end. That night camaraderie saved the day. Several of us sat on the floor in the hallway of our dorm and practiced splinting and bandaging, in preparation for a test the next day. We all laughed a lot, and I let myself forget about my paralyzed patient.

Spring arrived. Some of the girls headed to the rooftop of the dorm to tan. I didn't join them, because asphalt and rocks were not my thing, but I did join the soap opera crowd. A few days a week after class, we plopped on the couches in the living room in the old building to follow the continuing saga of *Another World*. We brought bags of chips and cans of soda and shamelessly devoured them as our eyes remained glued to the set. I also spent time in the so-called comic book room. The room belonged to a classmate who dressed and decorated in the *hippie* style. She hung beads in her doorway, burned incense and her room always looked like a tornado had rolled through. Supposedly, the housemothers sent her regular reminders to clean it, but it never changed. She was a chain-smoker and a clutter queen, but she was also bright and funny...*and* she always had a massive pile of comic books available for us to read. I enjoyed her company.

One day, after class, a couple of friends and I decided to explore the original hospital. We entered through the front door, which led into a large hall with a checkered black-and-white marble floor. A large reception desk just inside the door was empty. Billing offices occupied the first floor, but they were all closed for the day.

We climbed a large staircase with brass banisters behind the reception desk, heading up to the second floor. The upstairs hall opened onto several large rooms with floor-to-ceiling windows; each room contained about eight iron beds. The beds had cranks instead of the electric controls found in the new hospital. All the furniture in the rooms appeared to be antique. Only one room had a few elderly patients; all the other rooms were empty.

Our presence was eventually challenged by a little old nun. (Apparently, antique nuns cared for antique patients!) We told her we were nosy students. She was kind and allowed us to continue snooping.

We saw a kitchen that could have been from the 1920s and another small utility room off the hallway that was a place to empty bedpans. Everything smelled...old; I'm not sure how else to describe it. It was the odor of antique shops but there was something else in the air. Maybe it was residual cooking smells—or even the smells of people. I thought of the thousands of people who passed through the doors of this building. We finally made our way up to the attic. Here we found additional outdated equipment. But we enjoyed a twilight view of the downtown skyline.

When I did some research about the hospital and my nursing school, I found old newspaper clippings documenting the true original hospital opened a few blocks away in 1878 and was the first in the city. It was a two-story structure with twelve beds. The building across from the nursing school we toured replaced that structure in 1882 and had over two hundred beds. The nursing school was established in 1915. Nurses were trained in the hospital. The dorm was built in 1929.

We lost about ten percent of the class after the first year. A few students were academically challenged; others dropped out because they did not like nursing. The seventy remaining students were ready to rotate to specialty areas, such as the operating room, obstetrics, pediatrics, psychiatry—and the emergency room.

CHAPTER TWO

Obstetrics

———◆·———

Most of the students loved obstetrics, but I was not one of them. I thought labor and delivery looked and sounded like torture. The mothers labored in a common room; they were separated by curtains. The room was stark, with a linoleum floor, and noisy. I don't know if the mothers' cries were borne out of their pain or were the result of the medication they were given. Narcotics were frequently administered to the mothers, along with a medication for nausea called scopolamine. Some of the women seemed to almost hallucinate from this combo. One of the regular nurses told me the scopolamine was used to blunt the mothers' memory, so they would not remember the pain. There was a desk area with a blackboard for the nurses at one end of the room. The names and locations of every patient were listed on the blackboard, along with information about the status of each woman's labor. We recorded the dilation of the cervix, using a numeric value from 1 to 10, with 10 signifying that dilation was complete. We also recorded the baby's "station"—how far down the birth canal the baby's head had progressed. When dilation of the patient's cervix was "complete" it meant the birth would soon follow. Periodically, the labor and delivery nurses put on one glove then reached two fingers inside the mother to determine the dilation and the station progress, then they updated the information on the board. They knew when the patient was close to delivery and when to call the doctor. If the mother's personal doctor was not in the hospital, a resident was always available. Residents are doctors who have graduated from medical school but are still completing additional training. In years past they were known as interns. Students were not allowed to do cervical examinations. We observed, and we sometimes administered medications. We tried to soothe the mothers with words, and by applying damp washcloths to their foreheads. The natural childbirth movement had not yet reached our hospital, so no husbands or family members were in the labor room. It would be a few more years before significant others received permission to enter the inner sanctum of the maternity ward so they could be with their partners or spouses during labor or delivery.

When labor progressed to the delivery stage, the mother was wheeled to a private room, which had a tiled floor—and walls. She then was transferred to a padded steel table. Her legs were elevated, then bent at the knees and placed apart, into holders. A sheet was draped over her legs to just below the knees. There were straps to restrain her wrists.

It was my first delivery and I thought the table and the hand straps looked awful. I cringed when I watched the doctor make an incision in the patient's vagina to facilitate the delivery of the infant's head. This was called an *episiotomy*; it was performed routinely to reduce tearing during the birth process. There was a great deal of amniotic fluid as well as some blood; the baby came out looking wet and messy. This was normal. Pictures taken from the delivery room or the maternity ward always show a smiling mother holding a pink newborn in a blanket; what the pictures don't show is the nurses wiping the baby off.

The hospital offered a free clinic for women who were unable to pay for obstetrical care, and each student was assigned a patient to follow from this clinic. We each were introduced to our patient during her first trimester. Our assignment included teaching the patient about the changes she could expect in her body as her pregnancy progressed, and about the labor and delivery process. We accompanied the patient to her prenatal checkups, and we were expected to be present at their labor and delivery. That meant we were "on call" for the birth—which in turn meant we had to provide the housemother with a phone number where we could be reached if we left the dorm around the due date, since we did not have cell phones or beepers. The housemother would come to our dorm room and wake us up if the hospital called during the night. After the birth, we had to write a paper detailing the entire experience for our instructor. The paper would count for a portion of our final grade in the course.

My patient was an unmarried fifteen-year-old young woman. She had dropped out of school because of her pregnancy; now, she lived at home with her parents, awaiting the birth of her child. The family was in one of the lower socioeconomic tiers. I tried my best to educate the patient about her pregnancy, and I provided basic information about labor and delivery, but I was never certain how much she was able to grasp. Time would tell.

Late one afternoon, the housemother came to my room. My patient was in labor. I reported promptly to the hospital and found her thrashing and screaming intermittently. I was informed that the resident on duty was NOT generous with pain medication. One of the regular registered nurses (RNs) working in the labor room walked up to me and said, "Pray, little student, your patient goes fast, because that resident is not going to give her *anything.*" I tried a cool wash rag to my patient's forehead and soothing words, but neither was helpful. I was clueless as to what else I could offer her. I simply hoped things would conclude quickly.

Her labor did not go fast but the outcome was good: a healthy baby. I hoped the newborn's home situation would also be healthful, but with a high school dropout mother of little means, the situation did not look particularly promising. A home health nurse would probably visit the mother to assess the baby's growth and review basic infant care—but after that, mom and baby would be on their own.

At this time there was a private physician not associated with clinic patients who was heavy-handed when administering narcotics during labor. Babies delivered under his care sometimes experienced respiratory distress because of his practices. Nurses on staff whispered about his "blue babies." The physician was also notorious for the vaginal repairs he performed after delivery, which supposedly enhanced sexual pleasure after the mother recovered from the birth. He was called the Love Doctor. However, it seemed the special repair was not necessarily beneficial to women. Some of his patients had problems with urination due to swelling after the repair; they had to have a rubber tube called a catheter inserted into their bladders to drain their urine. The nurses on staff whispered that some women had long-term difficulties because of the surgery. It appeared the whisperings were credible: a story about the doctor appeared on a TV news show years later. I heard he voluntarily gave up his license, and the hospital suffered serious public relations damage. Supposedly a nurse was instrumental in bringing the physician's transgressions to light, but I was not able to confirm this part of the story. During the immediate postpartum period, the nurses palpated the lower abdomen of the mothers to make sure the uterus was firm and that no excessive bleeding was occurring. We administered medications for hemorrhoids or pain, if necessary. Throughout the first day after birth, the babies were transported to and from the mother's bedside, usually for feeding.

Fortunately, restraints and mind-altering drugs are no longer part of the birthing process. Shortly after graduation one of my nurse friends declined the episiotomy and gave birth without any difficulty or significant tearing. Today, in some hospitals, women can deliver their baby in the same private room where they undergo labor. The rooms look like hotel rooms with artwork and linens; the beds look like real beds, but the end of the bed drops down, and stirrups can be added for delivery. Fancy linens might be a marketing ploy, but the most important improvement that's been made since my days of nursing school is allowing husbands and significant others to stay with the mother throughout the entire labor and delivery process. Additionally, pain is so much better managed with epidural blocks instead of shots of narcotics. Today, some families bring video cameras. Years later, I laughed at a comment a coworker made when we were reliving some of the "finer moments" we had witnessed during childbirth. My coworker said her father-in-law *and* his video camera would NOT be welcome in her delivery room.The portion of the obstetrics rotation during which we cared for newborn babies was fun and gave me a warm, satisfying feeling. We spent a few weeks in the newborn nursery. We were taught a special way to wrap the baby with a blanket to calm the newborn; with the blanket wrapped around them, they looked like they were in a papoose. We put little knit caps on their heads because much of an infant's body heat is lost through the head. We taught the mothers how to hold and bathe their baby, and how to take their baby's temperature.

The babies stayed at their mother's bedside during most of the day in a plastic bed that rested on a metal frame with wheels. A card with their name was taped to the top of the plastic bed. The babies were returned to the nursery in the evening so their mothers could sleep. Breast fed babies were the exception; they were brought out every three to four hours during the night. The nurses bottle fed the other babies during the night with formula that came in four-ounce bottles prepared by the manufacturer.

A newborn's umbilical cord stump takes a week or two to dry and fall off. It always reminded me of a pumpkin stump. We cleaned it with the same tiny alcohol pads we used to prep a patient's skin for a shot. By now we had completed a full year of nursing school, and we were able to pick up paid time in the hospital after classes and on weekends. The hospital usually had open positions on the evening and night shifts, so they welcomed student nurses working this "free time." We reported to the nursing office, and a person on duty looked over a handwritten master sheet that listed each nursing floor and how many nurses were assigned to be on duty. The students were sent to the neediest areas. I was assigned to the nursery on a night shift in the dead of winter. I sat in a rocking chair, feeding a baby while looking out a window watching snowflakes drift by. I remember feeling happy and thinking it was really something to be paid for doing something I enjoyed so much. (What is it about newborns? They are *so* cute and smell *so* good—and it's not just the baby powder!)The hospital also had a neonatal care unit. This unit was a separate nursery from the normal newborn nursery. It provided a higher level of care for sick newborns; tiny premature infants were immediately transferred there. I could not believe the size of these infants; some of them were shorter than my forearm. They look wizened and discolored. Occasionally, full-term infants were transferred to the neonatal unit if they showed signs and symptoms of distress during birth. Their stay in the unit was usually brief. The stay for some of the tiny "preemies" could be prolonged and heart-wrenching as we struggled to keep them alive. Some preemies developed infections that could not be overcome with the drugs available at that time. Some had cerebral bleeds. During this rotation I saw an infant who was born missing certain cranial bones and another with intestines outside of the body. The babies were not expected to live; they were given palliative care. No one talked about medical ethics in relation to these cases, but at this point I had enough training and knowledge to start thinking, *How do we know if we're saving life or prolonging the inevitable?*

The weight of the premature infant and the number of weeks of gestation (the number of weeks the baby was *in utero*) were used to predict the infant's chances of survival. Predicted survival parameters have changed markedly over the years as the equipment has become more sophisticated.

The nurseries had anterooms where we scrubbed our arms and hands and put a gown over our clothing, so we would not bring in germs from the outside world. In the neonatal unit, most infants were inside an incubator instead of in an open crib. Some of the infants had tubes inserted in their mouths and were attached to respirators. They were fed intravenously, or else a tube was threaded down through their nose, into their stomach. The nurses attached a syringe with formula to the tube and let the nourishment slowly flow by gravity into the infant's stomach. The objective was to give the infant time for its body to grow and for its lungs to mature. We controlled the infant's temperature in the incubators because premature babies have very little body fat. If they become cold, they use energy and could need additional oxygen to generate warmth. We hoped to prevent infection while the infant was growing. The nurses on staff who worked in the unit tried to support the parents. But I was not aware of any special training for the nurses as they struggled to deal with the emotionally traumatized parents—or, even worse, the death of the baby.

CHAPTER THREE

Psychiatry

———————◆———————

Our textbook described and categorized numerous mental disorders. Obsessive compulsive behavior. Mania. Depression. Schizophrenia. The term *crazy* was unfortunately used in medical circles. Its use continues today, though not by mental health professionals. But I think there will always be some doctors and nurses who attribute symptoms or complaints they cannot explain or alleviate to a patient being "crazy." Over the years, I learned that the "craziest" symptoms can be caused by simple things like chemical imbalances, including vitamin and mineral deficiencies. I've learned that drugs, even over-the-counter medications, can contribute to an imbalance. I have also learned that people develop patterns of behavior to circumvent intolerable stress. Fortunately, doctors today seem to do a more thorough workup to rule out these other causes before making a diagnosis.

The definition of *psychosis* is "out of touch with reality." People who are psychotic hear or see things that that the rest of us do not. Their behavior is generally fearful. My frame of reference at the time was mainly constructed by movies like *Psycho* or *Hush... Hush, Sweet Charlotte*. And there were always those awful newspaper stories about serial killers, who I thought *must* be psychotic. Secretly, I feared that something could happen to one of us on the psych ward. As it turned out, I saw very few people who were out of touch with reality, and most of those patients had a substance abuse problem or were elderly and had dementia.

Hardening of the arteries was a popular explanation for why certain elderly patients we treated were out of touch with reality. A diagnosis of Alzheimer's did not exist yet. We frequently referred to these patients as "sundowners," because their symptoms seemed to escalate at night. Some were cute and childlike even though they were confused. The nursing assistants pampered them. They fixed the ladies' hair and shaved the men then parked them out in the hall, strapped to their wheelchairs with a cloth belt, so they could not wander. They jabbered at us as we went about our business up and down the halls. The family doctor rarely ordered psychiatric pills for them, and only did so if they were significantly disruptive. I don't know what the medical workup for providing a diagnosis of their condition was like in those days. We never questioned it. We just did our best to keep them clean, safe, and fed.

Today, a geriatric psychiatrist might be consulted and then the latest psychiatric pills would be ordered. I'm not certain if the new specialist and the new designer drugs really clear up confusion or improve quality of life in these patients. One thing is certain, however: patients no longer are belted in their wheelchairs in the halls of hospitals; this is considered abuse. Nurses used to have the authority to use restraints at their discretion to ensure a patient's safety. Today, a doctor must order any type of restraint and specify a time frame for its use. Personally, I think using a canvas belt to keep a patient from falling out of bed or a wheelchair is a good thing. During my time in the psychiatric ward, patients seemed to thoroughly enjoy sitting in the hall and observing the world. I also believe they remained more alert and even ate better when they were fed in the hall. Walk into some nursing homes today and you might see a patient's mattress on the floor, to prevent them from falling out of bed, since they can't be restrained. Never mind the back problems the medical staff members providing patient care "on the floor" might develop. It seems like common sense has left the practice of medicine in nursing homes.

Sometimes people with neurologic diseases somehow became intermingled with psychiatric patients. I remember one woman who wandered up and down the halls, swinging her arms in a fashion that almost mimicked a symphony conductor. She mumbled as she performed her maneuvers. It turned out that she was not psychotic; nor was she a substance abuser. She had a medical condition called Huntington's disease, a hereditary disorder that causes involuntary movements and mental deterioration. She was hospitalized on a locked ward.

Drug and alcohol withdrawal were usually managed on a designated psychiatric ward rather than on the medical floor. The designated ward looked very much like any other hospital floor, but the staff entered and exited through a locked door. The staff wore street clothes with lab coats; no white dresses and nursing hats. We gave shots of strong tranquilizers to help the addicted over the hump. We also used restraints—both cloth and leather—when the patients were hallucinating. Detoxing addicts were a supreme challenge and they behaved as described in our textbooks. They were disoriented regarding time and place, and they picked at their skin to remove crawly things that did not exist.

Depression was the most common diagnosis among the psychiatric patients we cared for, and we were taught the most peculiar way to communicate with these patients. We were not supposed to offer opinions or advice. For example, if a patient talked about his or her feelings or certain situations in his or her life, and then asked, "What should I do?" we were to reply, "What do you think you should do?" or "Tell me more." I found this odd. Obviously, the patients were depressed because they could not come up with a coping strategy that worked, and they wanted direction. I hoped their sessions with the psychologist or psychiatrist were more productive. Drug therapy was a significant part of their treatment. We administered drugs like lithium and tricyclics, which could have significant side effects. Patients could also attend workshops to make art or pottery. Electroshock therapy was considered somewhat of a last-ditch effort, when a patient was not improving by other means.

Electroshock therapy was administered in the freestanding mental health care building across the street from the nursing dorm. As had been the case during my obstetrical rotation, I was assigned a patient to follow and expected to write a paper about the experience which counted toward my final grade in the course. My patient was a man in his thirties. I don't remember much about him...just what we did to him.

Theoretically, electroshock therapy is supposed to reset the patient's brain—like resetting a clock—and thus lift the depression. I accompanied my patient to the treatment room. It looked a bit like an operating room seen on TV. The orderly and one of the staff nurses on the unit moved him to a table and applied straps to his arms and legs. A padded tongue blade was placed into his mouth. The nurse applied a special jelly to each side of his head, and tiny flat spoons were placed on top of the jelly; the spoons were held down by a rubber headband. Cords from the spoons attached directly to a machine. Someone yelled "Clear!"—meaning we were all to make certain we were not touching the patient or the table. Then someone, probably the attending doctor, pressed a button; an electrical shock was delivered to the patient's head. The shock elicited a brief convulsion, the reason the tongue blade had been placed in the patient's mouth. His entire body shook and jerked... it looked horrible. I had never seen a convulsion, much less one that was purposefully induced.

After the shock, the patient went into a deep sleep. We applied oxygen and monitored his pulse and blood pressure as he slept.

He awakened feeling no pain, so to speak, because he essentially had no short-term memory. He asked repeatedly where he was and what day and time it was. I was told this was a side effect of the treatment, and that it was only temporary.

I didn't know what to think. You can't be depressed if you can't remember—but who wants to be a blank? The patient did not come out of his fog while I was on duty that day. He was my assignment on the day of the procedure only, and I wasn't on duty to follow up on his condition the following day.

Our next assignment was at a children's psychiatric hospital. It was a few miles away and not part of our hospital system. The nursing school had contracts with some other facilities, so the student nurses could broaden their experience.

The different units within the facility were organized according to age and gender. The day before I began there, I silently pleaded to the powers above not to assign me to adolescent boys. I grew up with sisters, and I really didn't know how to deal with fistfights or rough language, which I imagined would be part of an assignment to this unit.

Of course, when the assignments were announced, I had been assigned to pre-adolescent boys.

The boys in my assigned unit ranged in age from about eight to twelve years old. Many were in the facility for problems with "impulse control," or so it was called at that time. Some had started fires or had killed animals. Others were diagnosed with manic depression, a condition characterized by episodes of euphoria and hyperactivity followed by depression and apathy. Today, the condition is known as bipolar disorder. I remember how shocked I was at the overall appearance of the ward, which I would describe as stark. The ward had bare, painted concrete block walls, with wooden tables and chairs, and a television. Nothing was "cushy" or seemed at all comfortable. No toys were visible, nor anything to do. Eventually, I was told toys were controlled so the patients could not harm themselves.

The sleeping quarters looked the same as the living room. There was also a small kitchen off the main living room area. I helped the boys make cereal and toast with apple butter for their breakfast.

After breakfast, the boys were directed to move the dining chairs into a circle and a therapist arrived and initiated a discussion. The therapist was a trained psychologist and used a group format to assess the mental status and progress of the residents. He came several times a week. Apparently, the psychiatrist who is a medical doctor showed up only once a week for the group discussion. I don't know if or when the psychiatrist gave individual attention to the patients. The group meeting was followed by designated indoor game time: board games appeared, as well as materials to make crafts or models. Later, there was designated outdoor playtime, and the boys were given balls. The play yard was surrounded by a very high chain-link fence, which reminded me of a prison. I absolutely couldn't believe it.

My role at the psychiatric hospital was mostly observation. I tried to be kind and join in some of the games. Curiously, I have no memory of parents—or anyone else—visiting the children. I don't know what the ward's visitation policy was, but I do remember thinking, *What comes first? Do you act up because you are not loved or noticed? Or are you unloved and ignored because you act up?*

Our psychiatric experience concluded with a few days of observation at the state-run adult psychiatric facility. It was another huge nineteenth-century building on a large fenced-in space in an older part of the city. The property and the building appeared ill kept. The so-called green space was generally brown, with some overgrown weeds. When I entered the building, I was in a large reception hallway, with the usual old marble floor and a desk. The actual wards where patients resided were in locked corridors off to each side of the reception area. I was assigned a patient, and I was again required to write a paper about my patient's diagnosis, my assessment of the patient's condition, and any nursing interventions I had taken. The paper would factor into my grade.

My patient was a middle-aged woman. I don't remember her diagnosis, but I do remember that when I went to her room to introduce myself, I was speechless. She was wearing nothing but a full slip. One of the straps was attached with a safety pin. She had no shoes or socks....Where were her clothes? Her room was bare except for a small nightstand and a twin bed with sheets and a pillow. She opened the drawer of the nightstand and pulled out the remnants of a piece of pie covered with a paper napkin. She offered me some. Despite her psychosis, whatever it was, the woman had not lost her manners.

Fast-forwarding years ahead, it was my turn to seek mental health care. As I drove around a parking lot beside beige stucco buildings looking for the counseling center, I felt frightened, almost panicked. I said to myself, "You are a nurse, for God's sake, why are you afraid?" The answer was my psychiatric experience in nursing school: it could be described only as surreal.

Also, the word around the campfire at the school was that some of the psychiatrists were not quite as "crazy" as the patients… but they were close.

CHAPTER FOUR

Surgery

————◆————

We walked through automated doors labeled "Surgery, Restricted Personnel Only." A woman in surgical "scrubs" attended to a large desk. Several telephones sat on the desk, and they were all ringing simultaneously. A board on the wall listed the room number for each operating room. The room number was followed by a surgeon's name, and both the starting time and the name of the procedure being performed. Another set of automated doors stood across from the desk, with a sign warning: *No Street Clothes Beyond this Point.*

We were required to enter a locker room and change into either a scrub dress or scrub pants and top. We pulled a pair of paper booties out of a box and put them on over our shoes. Finally, we put a paper hat like a shower cap over our head, making certain to cover all our hair. When we added a mask, we were finally ready to enter one of the operating rooms.

The corridor outside the operating rooms was tiled and brightly lit. The air was cold. There were sinks outside each operating room; they were controlled by foot pedals. Back in the classroom, we had been indoctrinated as to the sanctity of the operating room and the meaning of sterility. We were about to practice what we had learned.

We had learned how to scrub our hands and our arms to the elbow. Most importantly, we had learned how to rinse holding each arm up, so the dirty water ran toward our elbows. After scrubbing we put on a mask then donned a long-sleeved surgical gown, pulling it over our scrub clothes. The gown had been autoclaved, or run through a sterilizer. We completed our outfit by adding sterile gloves. Inevitably, my nose would itch when I had on the mask and gloves, and I was helpless to address the itch.

In the operating room fabric-wrapped trays of autoclaved instruments were sitting on stainless steel tables. There were specific trays of instruments for each operation. The nurses opened the trays when the surgeon arrived; once a tray was opened it was considered a sterile field. No one touched the contents of the sterile field except the surgeon or his assistants. If the surgeon requested additional materials, like sponges, gauze, or an additional surgical instrument, a nurse would open the relevant sterile package over the sterile field and drop the contents onto the tray without contaminating the item.

The trays of instruments were arranged daily. They passed through a steam or gas autoclave cycle to ensure sterility. A glass vial of bacteria was also run through the autoclave daily, to check if the sterilizer was performing as it should. The vial indicated whether conditions were met for sterilization to take place, but in order to ensure the instruments would be sterile, they had to be scrubbed off before they even went into the autoclave.

It seemed there were countless instruments. Seasoned nurses knew them all, and I was told it took almost a year to become a seasoned nurse in the operating room (OR). So, we would probably remember only a few of the names before our surgery rotation ended.

During an operation, a nurse or a surgical tech handed the instruments to the doctor. They also cut the ends of the suture as the doctor stitched. Another nurse, called a circulator, was available to obtain additional equipment or supplies as needed during the operation. The circulator also documented the proceedings, including the instrument and sponge count. Some of the doctors employed their own personal nurses or surgical techs to assist in surgery. If a hospital was a teaching facility, a resident might observe or assist in the surgery.

Our assignment was essentially observation. We were on "high alert" whenever we were near a sterile table. God forbid we would contaminate something! Some of the doctors enjoyed the audience and talked to the students throughout the operation. Some tolerated us and were humorless and authoritative. I enjoyed the commentary and applauded these people, who could stand in place for such long periods of time, staying focused on the intricate task of dissecting and patching. I thought they had to have basket-ball-sized bladders.

The anesthesiologist played an important role during surgical operations. He or she reviewed the patient's medical history and determined the most appropriate drugs to give the patient. That was an important function, because there were—and there still are—options regarding anesthesia. Sometimes a spinal anesthetic is used instead of a general anesthetic. A patient takes longer to recover after receiving a spinal anesthetic, but a spinal anesthetic is considered safer for people with bad lungs. During my rotation, one anesthesiologist was assigned for each operation, start to finish. Today, an anesthesiologist usually sits through only the high-risk cases. They supervise the nurse anesthetists who deliver the anesthesia.Before any surgery the OR nurses made certain patients were correctly positioned and padded so that the patient's nerves would not be damaged during the operation. The area of the patient's body that was being operated upon was draped so that only the place where the incision would be made was visible. Before making the incision, the surgeon or the surgical assistant cleaned the surgical site with gauze dipped in an antibacterial liquid. The liquid was usually an iodine product; it stains the skin brown. The number of instruments, sponges, and sharps (needles and scalpels) was counted before a procedure started and when the procedure was finished. Leaving an instrument or a sponge in a patient is a nightmare! I can't figure out how this happens, if procedures are followed correctly. Years after graduating nursing school, when I attended a risk management conference, I saw multiple X-rays clearly showing instruments left inside patients!

Sometimes during an operation music would be playing softly in the background. If the surgery was easy and routine, the staff might chatter among themselves about everyday life.

One winter morning we awakened to a blizzard. This was not a problem for the student nurses, because we used the underground tunnel to walk over to the hospital, but most of the OR staff was late or no shows, so the plan was to use the students in a more active role during the routine "minor" operations, like a simple hernia repair. The surgeon in the room where I was assigned would have none of this. He took one look at me and the other student and barked, "You call this 'help'? Call off surgery."

I wasn't offended. I was ready to move onto my next rotation. The OR didn't seem to be the career choice for me...because I felt intimidated and uncomfortable around many of the surgeons.

CHAPTER FIVE

Pediatrics

The bad news about our pediatric rotation was we had to commute to another hospital during morning rush hour *and* find our own transportation to get there. There were no buses. My parents let me take the family's second car to school for part of this rotation. My sisters and I shared the second car. The good news was the place was new, looked beautiful, and (I swear) smelled just like baby powder. Also, the pediatrics instructor was a very nice nun who reportedly gave lots of As. I soon learned that caring for a child who was a pediatric patient was a lot easier then interacting with the child's parents.

A child could have received the most devastating diagnosis and still be in the playroom totally engrossed and oblivious to everything. I would see an eight-year-old boy giggling at a comic book even though he was immobilized, with a leg swinging in traction. Little tots with bald heads caused by chemotherapy were riding tricycles in the hallway.

Administering medication to a small child was usually a monumental challenge. We were taught some creative ways to accomplish this task. We put medications in pudding or applesauce, and sometimes we squirted liquid medication into the sides of their mouth with a syringe that didn't have a needle. It took at least one, and sometimes two, additional staff members to hold them still for an injection. I hated to make them cry, but crying was inevitable after an injection.

The most important lesson I learned on this rotation was that the leading cause of death in children over the age of one year was unintentional injury. We learned about the developmental milestones in children and how they related to safety. Preaching safety was part of our job.

Parents often had a double burden: they worried about their sick child *and* they felt guilty about neglecting their other children at home. There were no good answers for this psychological trauma. I understood that this was a reason some of the parents had short tempers. I knew it would take me longer than this single rotation to develop a smooth communication style for upset parents.

I liked pediatrics but succumbed to my first real illness while on this rotation. I went home to my parents' house for the weekend with a fever and belly pain. My dad drove me to the local emergency room (ER). The doctor didn't think I had appendicitis and sent me back home. I stayed in bed all weekend with shaking chills and lower gastrointestinal (GI) distress. On Monday, I returned to school and went to the student health clinic. The doctor there looked at me and said, "You are admitted." I was wheeled to the hospital via the tunnel and placed in isolation. An intravenous (IV) drip was started, and a nurse came in with a cup and told me to poop in it; this happened right in front of my boyfriend, who was visiting at the time! I was mortified.

It turned out several other students were also sick and had been admitted with the same problem. We later learned we all had the same bacterial infection, which could be spread by contaminated food or dirty hands. I was reminded again about the importance of hand washing after cuddling kids and changing diapers.

I did get an A in the course. So, did most of the class.

CHAPTER SIX

The Emergency Department

The emergency department had recently been remodeled and was considered state-of-the-art. The medical personnel working there seemed to be in perpetual motion. The main room had six stretchers separated by curtains. The emergency squad delivered people to the main room. The stretchers were designated for people with difficulty breathing, active bleeding, chest pain, or abdominal pain. These complaints could mean a potentially life-threatening condition. Each stretcher had a heart monitor mounted on the wall next to it and a large overhead light. There was also a chair in the corner of the room called the ENT (ear, nose, and throat) chair. We used it for ear and throat complaints, and for patients with nosebleeds. It looked like a chair in a dentist's office.

A larger observation room was down the hallway from the main room of the emergency department. It had ten beds and was used as a holding spot for people who had been seen in the main room and were waiting for tests to be performed on them. It was also used for people with less serious complaints, such as fevers, back pain, or what we called "female problems." Sometimes, if the hospital was full and a patient needed to be admitted to a room, the patient stayed in this area overnight. The nurses provided these patients with a basin of water and a toothbrush so they could freshen up in the morning. We also provided a breakfast tray, if they were able to eat. Most of the nurses preferred the main room over the back room; they wanted to be where the action was. We took turns working the two rooms. There was also an orthopedic room, where splints and casts were applied. There was one small room, which looked like a room in a private doctor's office; it had an examining table that converted to a table for gynecologic examinations.

The nurses prepared the patients to be seen by the doctor. They helped the patients undress, then took their temperature, pulse, and blood pressure; they also put the appropriate equipment on a stand next to the stretcher. Patients who complained of chest pain were hooked up to a cardiac monitor.

After examining a patient, the doctor gave the nurses orders regarding the patient's treatment. A nurse would start the intravenous infusion (if the doctor had ordered it), administer medication, and complete the paperwork for any lab tests that needed to be done or any X-rays that had to be taken. Desktop computers were not around; paperwork was completed by hand. We picked up the phone and summoned the lab or a tech to perform an electrocardiography (EKG). Generally, one nurse followed the same patient until he or she was discharged, but it was a team effort when a patient came in with a life-threatening condition.

The squad arrived with a young woman who had been involved in an automobile accident. She was covered in blood. Blood also oozed through the gauze the squad personnel had taped to her face. Most of the staff dropped what they were doing and came to the patient's stretcher. One of the nurses took her blood pressure while another cut off her clothes so we could identify any sites that were actively bleeding. Her limbs appeared normal and her abdomen had no open wounds, but the doctor said her abdomen was hard—a sign of internal bleeding. Someone picked up the phone and told the operator to page X-ray, the lab, and a surgeon, STAT. The word *stat* means "come immediately we have a serious situation." One of the nurses removed the gauze from the woman's face. There was a gash through her cheek so deep we were able to see inside her mouth; it was a sight I never imagined. We started intravenous fluid in both arms, trying to flood her with fluid because her blood pressure was dropping and now was dangerously low. She was awake but couldn't talk. Her eyes were filled with fright; her body was obviously pumping adrenaline to compensate for the blood loss.

Our efforts were too little and too late. She lost her blood pressure shortly after arrival and stopped breathing.

Someone immediately picked up the phone and informed the operator there was a Code 99 in Emergency Room Three. Code 99 signifies a life-and-death situation. The operator broadcast the information hospital wide over the intercom. This brought the residents, a nursing supervisor, and respiratory technicians with a respirator. The ER doctor inserted a plastic tube down the patient's throat to provide oxygen to her. The nurses administered multiple doses of adrenaline intravenously between attempts to try to jump-start her heart with the electric paddles. Another form of electricity was in the air that day, too—the anxiety and excitement arising from the motions and emotions of the staff. I could feel my heart beating fast.

We worked on the patient for almost an hour, but it was no use. The doctor suddenly stopped the controlled chaos around the bed and said the words: "Call it." Someone looked at the clock and pronounced the time of death.

That day, I knew I wanted to work in the emergency room. The blood didn't bother me, although helping to prepare the body for the coroner was horrible, especially because the patient was so young, and she had arrived at the ER alive. To prepare the body, we used a package called a morgue pack. It contained a white plastic sheet to wrap the body in, string, and two tags. One tag went on the deceased's chest and the other on one of her toes. The nurses rolled the wrapped body onto another metal cart with a false top for transport to the morgue. I remember the hollow sound the body made as it hit the cart, because the cart had no mattress to absorb the noise.

I learned an important lesson that day: *Make it only a task, don't question or think about it.* I created a concrete storage box in my mind, so I had somewhere to file what happened that day, it was that painful.

Fortunately, most emergencies are not life threatening. We saw patients in the ER who had stomachaches, ear pain, coughs, and colds. We treated numerous sprains, broken bones, and cuts. The ER doctor stitched simple cuts. For this procedure, the nurses first set up a bedside tray with the basic instruments the doctor needed to stitch the cut and then asked him or her for their preference regarding the type and gauge of "thread," called suture material. Silk or nylon sutures were commonly used at that time. If the cut went through muscle or tendon, or if a patient did not have normal sensation in the body part where the cut was, a specialist was consulted. Deep wounds over joints were usually repaired in the operating room because the ER was not considered sanitary.

Eye injuries and nosebleeds were common among patients in the ER. After the ER doctor examined a patient who had an eye injury, a nurse would apply ointment and patch the eye. We always tried to stop nosebleeds with manual pressure, which we applied by pinching the patient's nostrils together for several minutes. If that did not work, the physician would pack the nose with gauze. If the patient was still significantly oozing blood after the packing, we called an ear, nose, and throat specialist.

Asthmatics were frequent ER visitors, particularly when seasons changed or the weather turned cold. The standard treatment at the time was three tiny doses of adrenaline administered by injection in the patient's arm; the doses were given five minutes apart. The patient also received some IV fluid with medication to dilate the respiratory passageways in the lungs. Today, the patients are given an aerosolized treatment. They are handed a small cup with a mouthpiece; it is attached by plastic tubing to a machine.

The cup contains liquid medication to dilate the airway passages. The machine blows air over the medication in the cup making a mist that can be inhaled. Adrenaline shots are no longer given; that form of treatment has fallen out of favor because of it caused the pulse rate to go up and the patient to become anxious. Children with high fevers were also brought into the ER. To reduce their fever, we filled metal pans with lukewarm water and swabbed the children down. The parents could have done this at home, but they didn't, because whenever a child has a fever and a parent tries to swab them the child cries and resists. In the ER, we ignored the crying. Instead, we simply did what was best for the child. Children do not tolerate high temperatures, and a child can have a seizure associated with his or her fever. These seizures are called febrile seizures. We also administered acetaminophen, employing the method we learned during our pediatric rotation: using a syringe without a needle, we squirted the medication into the side of the child's mouth.Being able to offer an immediate solution for some ER patients was gratifying. Even with other patients, for whom no immediate solution was available, I still found satisfaction by providing help and hope.

Frail, elderly patients came into the ER with a limp arm, a limp leg, or slurred speech—the signs of a stroke. They would be admitted for stabilization and rehabilitation. Other ER patients exhibited signs of a heart attack on their electrocardiogram (the graph produced by an EKG); they were also admitted.

During my rotation in the ER, I began to *really* apply the pieces of information memorized from my textbooks to the patients in front of me. I was learning what questions to ask the patients about their symptoms. I was able to start associating symptoms with body systems, and I was gaining a better understanding of diagnostic tests.

Part of our ER rotation was a trip down to the morgue to observe an autopsy. Watching a body being disassembled and its organs being weighed was horrific, but to me the most intolerable aspect of the autopsy was the smell. I was so revolted by the odor that to this day I have a hard time watching TV shows with scenes of autopsies.

Autopsies were performed more frequently a few decades ago, to confirm the cause of a patient's death. Sometimes, the presumed cause of death was found to be incorrect. Today, sophisticated scanners have reduced the number of autopsies. Autopsies are still performed in cases of unexpected death, when the patient had no known history of underlying disease. They are also performed when trauma is involved, or if a crime associated with the death is suspected.

The ER rotation concluded with time in the free clinic area. It was adjacent to the ER and was the same place where I had been introduced to my case study during my obstetrical rotation. The free clinic offered routine office care and ER follow-up, in addition to obstetrical care. The rooms were like any doctor's office. I was excited for the opportunity to be a real nurse, assisting patients instead of just observing doctors. The residents in the hospital rotated through the area; we would be assigned to follow one of them for a few days. Some of the residents were single…maybe, I thought, a Dr. Joe Gannon would be among them? In fact, while we waited for our assignment the first day, we overheard one resident say to another, "I get the cute one." Apparently, they were looking all of us over, too. I started to think maybe I wasn't ready to make a lifetime commitment to my high school boyfriend. Because who wouldn't want to marry a doctor?

CHAPTER SEVEN

Senior Year

————◆————

1971

We were officially seniors, so we packed our belongings and transported them on carts to the senior dorm in the old building. I recalled being told there was some benefit to living there, but for the life of me I couldn't think what it was.

I now had a private dorm room, but it wasn't one of the larger ones, and the furniture was dark and old, exuding a familiar odor. *Mildew.* The single window faced west, making the room incredibly hot. There was still no air-conditioning, and the box fan I set in the window was essentially worthless. I hoped my months would pass quickly.

At the hospital, we were rotating through the intensive care unit (ICU) and the coronary care unit (CCU). The two areas claimed a dozen monitor beds between them. Patients had to be clinically unstable to be on a monitor. Today, monitors are available throughout entire floors of hospitals and are used even for patients who have had abnormal heartbeats for decades and who are clinically stable. I'm uncertain whether studies have shown any benefit to this costly practice. Anyone can learn to hook up a patient to a monitor and learn the names of the configurations on the monitor. Assessing the patient's clinical condition in relation to the information displayed on the monitor screen—and knowing when to intervene—takes a lot more training and practice. We had a crash course on how to interpret the waveforms but becoming competent and confident in assessing the critically ill requires a lot more time than our rotation provided.

At the time of my senior year, patients diagnosed with a heart attack stayed in the hospital for over a week. They were on complete bed rest: they weren't allowed to get up for showers or even to walk over to their chair during their first few days in the hospital. They were treated like fragile glass. Today, a patient with a heart attack is expected to be discharged after three days, unless the patient has a significant complication like arrhythmia (abnormal heart rhythm) or abnormal blood pressure. There no longer are restrictions on bathing or shaving, which are allowed once the patient is stable and no longer receiving intravenous medication.

After our introduction to critical care, we returned to the medical and surgical floors to practice nursing management. This meant we were responsible for more than the two or three patients we were usually assigned. We were the nurse in charge of a team of patients, or half the patients on any given floor. We were responsible for phoning or paging a physician if a problem or change in condition in any of the patients arose. We accompanied the physicians when they visited the patients during their rounds. We administered the medications to the patients on our team. We supervised the care given by the nursing assistants and the other nurses on the team. At the end of our shift, we dictated notes into a tape recorder, detailing the highlights of all the patients on our team. We were almost fully fledged nurses, and it felt very good.

Most of us obtained even more practical experience by working in the hospital for pay during our off hours. This was how many of us paid off the debt we had assumed when we started nursing school.

One evening shift I was assigned to one of the orthopedic floors. As it happened, no registered nurses were available to work on the floor that night, so four senior students were assigned to the unit. The house nursing supervisor was available as a resource and made frequent stops at patients' bedsides. We were well trained, and I am proud to say there were no problems on our floor that night.

Back at the dorm, the radio was blaring.

> *Kisses and love won't carry me*
> *Till you marry, Bill.*
> *Bill, I love you so....*

One of the girls on my floor hung her freshly washed "good" undies in front of the hall window. She probably had a date. Cooking smells wafted through the halls, and some of my dormmates were socializing in the lounge. My nursing dorm felt like home…regardless of the mildew.

Around this time, gossip was running rampant about a real soap opera that had occurred at the hospital. A married surgical nurse had become romantically involved with one of the residents. When the nurse appeared in court for her divorce hearing, her soon-to-be ex-husband jumped up and stabbed her. The nurse was transported to our ER. She was in serious condition, with a punctured lung but was expected to recover.The situation created quite an uproar! The hospital was a Catholic institution; I heard the nurse was either suspended or fired, I don't recall which. The doctor continued to work so no one was sure what if anything was even said to him. Because of this incident, I began to wonder, *Were there different conduct standards for doctors and nurses?*

CHAPTER EIGHT

Graduate Nurse

———◆———

1972

The hospital promised every member of the graduating class a job. We were asked to submit a paper request identifying our shift and unit preference. No day shifts were available in the emergency department—and I wanted a day shift. So I accepted a position on a medical floor. It was a good starting point for any nurse.

Two of my friends and I decided to take a trip to Florida as a graduation present to ourselves. We drove to Disney World then continued down the east coast to infamous Fort Lauderdale, the spring break capital. We stayed in junky, sandy motels. We bar-hopped and danced the night away. We continued south to see the Everglades then drove up Florida's west coast on our way home. We were in a swimming pool in St. Petersburg when we suddenly noticed several senior citizens wearing winter coats were standing at poolside and shaking their heads at us. They couldn't believe anyone was swimming when the temperature was in the high sixties. We didn't care; we were deepening our tans before returning to work.

On my first day of work, I wore my graduation uniform and my nursing cap with the brown velvet stripe. On all the medical documentation I signed my name to, I would use the designation "GN"— Graduate Nurse—after my name. I would become an RN—Registered Nurse—when I passed the state board. I punched a time clock in the basement of the hospital. My starting pay was $3.82 an hour—less than what my sister made working as a waitress when tips were factored in. Incredibly, reporting to work early was discouraged; we were not to clock in earlier than seven minutes before our shift officially started because they did not want to pay us for the extra time.

Medical and surgical floors typically had twenty-eight to thirty-six beds. The hospital operated at full capacity most of the year, except during the summer. We practiced team nursing; the floor was "divided" in half, with three or four staff members on each team. On the weekend, a team might dwindle to two members. A team was always headed by an RN. The other team members might be another RN, an LPN (licensed practical nurse), or an NA (nursing assistant).

LPNs complete a one-year training program. At my hospital, they helped give medications and performed treatments like changing bandages. The scope of their practice was limited: they could not administer medications intravenously or receive doctor's orders over the phone. Today, the role of LPNs has expanded, most certainly for economic reasons.

When I was working as a GN, the NAs received on-the-job training. Today, most NAs complete a formal training program and take a certification test. NAs take patients' temperatures, help with bedpans, give baths, pass food trays, and feed patients. Most floors in my hospital had a unit secretary to answer the phone and fill out test requisitions, which were done by hand, as this was the era before hospitals—before the *world*, really—had desktop computers.

RNs assessed patient conditions and contacted physicians, as indicated. They reviewed all doctors' orders to make certain they were completed. They gave all medications including IV medications and recorded this on the patient's chart. They recorded an assessment of the patient's condition on the chart. They gave reports to the oncoming shift. They also performed treatments like bandage changes (if there was no LPN on their floor) and helped with clerical duties if a secretary wasn't available.

All the oncoming nurses listened to a recorded report about each patient from the charge nurse of the previous shift. The report included the patient diagnosis, any abnormal vital signs exhibited by the patient, complaints of pain, problems with mobility, status of any wounds (if the patient was postoperative), and the results of any pertinent tests. We took notes on our assigned patients and carried them in the pocket of our uniform to use as a frame of reference. The nurse team leader took notes on all the patients on her team and was the "go to" person if the doctors had any questions. At the end of a shift the RNs wrote a synopsis of each patient's day and gave the information to the charge nurse, so she could tape her report.

As the GN on my floor, I visited the patients room by room at the start of my shift. I'm a people person so I genuinely enjoyed greeting my patients and getting a feel for who they were. I also learned from my patients: What symptoms to expect with certain diseases. What treatments worked and did not work for them. During my first few months, I also watched—and learned from—the older nurses. I admired their patience and good humor.

I studied (a little) for the upcoming state boards. But I thought I was l prepared.

State boards were offered twice a year. The testing site was a building at the state fairgrounds. It was winter, and our examination room was freezing cold, so many of us wore our coats while taking our tests. We did not think of complaining. The rules were so strict that we were not even allowed to go to the bathroom without being accompanied by a hall monitor to ensure there was no cheating. After the test, we waited about two months for our results. I passed, as did almost the entire class. I was proud that I had achieved a high enough score to practice in any state (through a policy known as reciprocity). I exchanged my GN name badge for a badge that said RN. Registered Nurse.

As with any job, there were good times and bad times when I worked as an RN. The phone was always ringing—an unsteady patient would be trying to get out of bed. Blood pressures were too high or too low. Or else a patient was throwing up. Sometimes, patients developed rashes, so their doctor had to be contacted to address their medication. We dealt with stressed families, and we put a lot of mileage on our feet. But there were humorous times as well. I remember a dedicated (and very loud) proctologist. He was short, dumpy…kind of reminded me of the Penguin on *Batman*. You couldn't miss him when he visited your floor.

People sometimes ask me how I could be a nurse…but who sits in school and decides to be a butt doctor? One day, the proctologist stood in the nursing station bellowing about one of his patients who had recently undergone an operation for hemorrhoids and who was on our floor because the surgical floor was full. The proctologist shouted, "Who ordered iron tablets on my patient? It's like running a Mack truck over fresh cement." We all had a good laugh, because iron is *very* constipating. We all knew some resident's ass was grass.People occasionally went into delirium tremens (DTs) on our medical floor. This happened because we didn't always know who was alcoholic upon admission, and patients often were in denial. I watched one man become very disruptive when his doctor arrived. The doctor ordered an injection of a tranquilizer. I prepared the medication. A doctor and an orderly flanked me as I approached the bed with the tranquilizer. The doctor was a large man—but so was the patient. He sat up and shoved the doctor several feet backward….*Yikes!* We called for reinforcements. With a collective effort we were able to hold the patient down long enough for me to inject the medication.The cancer patients were very challenging to care for. I was again faced with trying to initiate cheery conversation with someone who was dying and knew it. I had no recollection of this situation being addressed during my training.

These patients often looked like the people in photographs of concentration camps. Medicating them was the absolute worst part of caring for these patients. Narcotics to treat pain were given by shot in those days, and there was no muscle or fat left on their bodies. I don't have the words to describe what it feels like to hit bone with the tip of a syringe. Thankfully, these days narcotics are administered intravenously or are given topically, rubbed onto the skin like a body cream; patients can now also lick a narcotic "lollipop." I was just adjusting to my new career when my high school boyfriend and I broke up. We had broken up before, but I knew this time was for good. A new orderly was assigned to my unit, and we kept running into each other. Even though he wasn't a doctor I thought he was very cute, so I accepted his invitation for a date. After a few dates, I found out he was a Vietnam veteran and kept a gun under his bed. I was totally put out about the gun and his paranoia. We never had guns in the house I grew up in, and the fact that the orderly had a gun was frightening to me, and it was my reason for retreating from the relationship. I truly did not understand the Vietnam experience those guys went through.

I missed the action and adrenaline rush of the ER. So, after a few months on the medical floor, I asked the nursing supervisor if any positions were open in the emergency department. One day he told me there was one and asked me to complete a transfer request.

I was thrilled.

CHAPTER NINE

Return to the ER

———•◆•———

The hospital's ER saw approximately 40,000 patients a year, or about 110 patients per day. We didn't have a triage system in place, but the staff in the admission office were trained to bring all charts with complaints of chest or abdominal pain directly to a nurse, so they could be called back immediately. Patients sometimes had a difficult time distinguishing between the two, and I learned what questions to ask to better determine what was going on. I took cardiac classes to improve my knowledge about reading a cardiac monitor, and I was trained to start IVs. The ER nurses started their own IVs and did not use the hospital IV team.

To treat patients with chest pain, ER nurses always started a small bag of dextrose (sugar water). The IV drip was run slowly, which is known as keeping a vein open. This technique was used so abnormal heart beats, which are often associated with heart attacks, could be promptly treated with medication. Patients having an asthma attack were typically given IV fluid containing medications to help open up their respiratory passageways. Two IVs were sometimes started on trauma victims who were bleeding and needed fluid replacement to help restore their blood pressure. I watched and learned from *everyone*: doctors, patients, other nurses. I was somewhat cocky. I was still too dumb to know how much I didn't know. The staff worked well together. The regular day shift ER physician was the boss of all the ER physicians; he was a nice and patient man. There was a family atmosphere; one quiet afternoon after my shift was over, the ER physician even pierced my ears. One ER physician was particularly interesting and entertaining. He was a black man who had been an English teacher in a previous life, before he became a physician. What I liked about him was that he always checked the age, gender, and occupation of his patients before he saw them, and he was able to make some accurate diagnostic predictions based just upon this information. He was easygoing and sometimes interjected apt literary quotes. To a female patient with abdominal pain he admonished, "You know, if you hadn't eaten those ribs yesterday, you wouldn't be here." The information about the ribs had not been offered by the patient, but it was accurate. After diagnosing a sexually transmitted disease in another patient, he quietly told the nurses, "It is better to have loved and lost than to have never loved at all." He also coined the term "snoopervisor" for the nursing supervisor. At times it was a very fitting description.

There were some physicians I did not like. One routine day I had been assigned to the back room in the ER. It was filled with several patients who had abdominal pain and back pain. They were all waiting for lab tests and the results of their X-rays. A big cheese in the obstetrics/gynecology department—middle aged, white hair, a bit paunchy—was walking around the unit, looking for a patient we did not have. He walked up to me and asked if he could speak to me in another room. Once we were in the room, he closed the door and said, "How about a kiss for an old man on his birthday?" He grabbed me and stuck his tongue in my mouth. I was appalled. I pushed him away before bolting out of the room to the nurse's lounge.

An older, wiser nurse saw me running, upset, into the lounge. She followed me there, and we talked. I told her what happened and considered my options. I decided to say nothing. This occurred in the 1970s: he was well known and respected…and I was a nobody new nurse. My friend and coworker said she would take care of it. I have no idea what she said or did, but I never saw him again in the ER.

A drunk was brought in by the squad; we saw lots of them. Whenever I took a whiff of one of them, I remembered what the diagnosis "grip of the grape" meant. Sometimes, that was all we could find wrong with them: drunk from cheap wine. But on that day, the squad said they had been called because this patient had suffered a seizure on the street. After he was transferred to the ER cart we began to peel off his layers of clothing. He was wearing his closet, as most street people do. As we hit the last layer we came in for a surprise. He had been shot. The wound was superficial, but it served to reinforce the axiom, always undress patients and look them over.

Another day, a young woman was brought in by the squad; she was in a stupor, and she was probably on drugs. The squad said she was a dancer at a local club. We were getting her undressed when I noticed her breasts were standing straight up. They didn't flatten out, even though she was lying flat on her back. *How peculiar,* I thought. They were also very big. And that was when I first realized what fake boobs look like. She also had noticeably long eyelashes. The glue holding them in place was also noticeable, and part of the lashes on one of her eyes was peeling off. The ER doctor came in just as we were getting a gown on her. He looked at the patient and immediately said, "The first thing we need to do is an eyelashectomy. I had to stifle a laugh.

The night shift nurses regularly complained to the day shift about the substandard performance of two of the doctors on their shift. There was a language barrier: the two doctors were from the Middle East, did not speak English very well and seemed to have a difficult time obtaining patient histories. But, more importantly, the nurses said they sometimes had to suggest treatment orders to these physicians. Experienced ER nurses know what tests and medications are usually ordered in response to patient conditions or complaints.

The nurses repeatedly passed on their concerns to their nursing supervisors, which was the appropriate chain of command at the time. Nothing was ever done. We figured night shift physicians were hard to come by: they were bodies with degrees. I filed the incident away and kept my mouth shut. Fortunately, this situation probably would not occur today, because working in the ER has become a medical specialty. Today, emergency physician groups vie for hospital contracts and report to the hospital's CEO—who, of course, reports to a board. If the ER physicians don't perform well, they might lose their contract. The power of the "good old boy" network has been significantly diminished.

Sometime during my first year in the ER, a doctor came around and asked me and several other the nurses if we would be interested in making ten dollars an hour putting "Band-Aids" on patients. He was a family doctor who moonlighted at General Motors as a facility physician. All big auto plants had a nurse on duty for each shift, and General Motors was apparently having difficulty filling their weekend evening shift. I jumped at the chance; the salary was astronomical compared to my hospital salary. The money would buy some much-needed furniture.

What a great opportunity! I learned how to examine an eye for a corneal abrasion and how to perform minor stitching. I practiced on a real pig's foot and wasn't even bothered by the sight of it.

I also got a firsthand look at America at work. The production area was very noisy, sometimes deafening. Employees wore earplugs. The plant was hot and smelled like motor oil and metal. The medical office was small, but the noise from the production floor was muted.

I had a lot of customers on my first few shifts. Most had minor complaints: abrasions, superficial cuts, headaches, backaches. I had standing orders to give the workers aspirin, and to apply antibiotic creams to cuts and scrapes. No one seemed to be in any real distress. Some of the workers were probably taking a break, or just curious: I was a new nurse. All of them were nice and polite, and I enjoyed talking with them.

When I received my first patient who needed stitches, I was scared to death. Everything went smoothly, though, from injecting the local anesthetic to stitching up the wound. I was proud! Sewing up people isn't that difficult; but it's a learned skill, like anything else. I didn't know it at the time, but some big city hospital ERs (not mine) were regularly using specially trained nurses or physician assistants to stitch wounds. I had to keep a log of all patient visits, including each patient's complaint and the treatment I administered. I also scheduled a follow-up appointment with the company physician, if it was indicated. If the problem was not work-related, patients were referred to their family doctor for follow-up.

At the hospital ER, nurses kept a log of a different sort: a spiral notebook entitled "Best Chief Complaints." I once recorded a complaint of "hole in head, baby in stomach, wants X-rays and medicine." Whew! Someone told this to the clerk, and she typed it out word for word. I noted the doctor of record was Dr. None—the most popular doctor in the inner city. The hospital knew that most patients we treated were poor and did not have a family doctor. So the hospital had an "on call" system to address this. The physicians on staff took turns being on call. This meant they would accept patients who did not have a doctor for follow-up. The patient was given the on-call doctor's name, address, and phone number...but it didn't mean the patient could, or would, make the call. For most of them, getting transportation to and from the doctor's office was a serious issue. It had never crossed my mind, until I realized that patients had difficulty just finding a ride home from the ER. Only one charity with a van gave rides. At times, we begged the nursing supervisor to provide cab fare. Patients primarily used city buses for transportation, and I had to wonder how many buses went out to the suburbs, where the private doctors practiced.

The auto plant offered me a full-time job on the 3-11 shift. Despite the higher hourly pay, I still liked working in a hospital better than working at the plant, and I didn't want to be tied down with a full-time evening job. So, I declined. I told my friend and coworker—the one who took care of the "problem doctor" for me—about the job. She was a single mom and jumped at the chance. I was happy for her.

It was a bad day. Not being a morning person had come back to bite me. Someone informed me that the pants to my pants suit were on inside out. I had been at work for almost two hours before I was made aware of my mistake! It was going to be one of those days when I spend my half-hour lunch taking a brief nap on the plastic couch in the lounge. I had done way too much bar hopping the previous night, and even young nurses can get worn out from the ER pace.

He was dark haired, with a receding hair line. And, he was on the stocky side. He was also a few years older than the other residents in his group. He was smart and perfectly comfortable offering words of wisdom instead of a prescription—which most patients had come to expect. He was also entertaining, and the only doctor I ever worked with who would shake his head during a particularly trying day and say, "Is it time to go home yet?" He became a teasing friend. When a member of his resident group asked me out one day while he was in hearing distance, he came over to me and quietly said, "Are you really going to go out with that schmuck?" Then one day he asked me to the ER Christmas party. I immediately said "yes" then added, "I thought I was going to have to go with the girls." He laughed at that.

My neighbor and I liked to sew, and she helped me make my dress. I went to the ball in my long, green velvet gown.... I felt like a princess.

I had a great time. Back at work, I suddenly really looked at him and thought I might be in love. Days later, at work, he caught up with me in the hall and put a small box in my hand. Then, he walked away.

I went to the lounge and opened the box; it contained a silver bracelet. I did not know what to think or do. Our relationship was fun and easygoing...and suddenly I was red faced and tongue tied around him. Additionally, another one of my nurse coworkers had a crush on him; after the Christmas party, she made life miserable for me at work.He never called me after the party...or after he gave me the bracelet. I was devastated. The hospital chaplain came up to me unsolicited and told me the doctor was smitten. I took his observation as a very positive development. But the ensuing positive outcome never happened; he didn't call.

It has been over thirty years. I still have the rhinestone barrettes I wore, and the silver bracelet. But the doctor got away.

All my high school friends were getting married, and I decided to change my life and move to the big city, Cincinnati. It was only an hour's drive from home, but it felt like a world away.

A guy was sitting on his balcony in my new apartment building when I pulled into the parking lot. He introduced himself and helped me carry some things in. Everyone in the building knew each other, and they were all young single folks, like me. There was a social worker, a chemist, and even a pianist who performed at night at a local bar. There was always someone to hang with, and it was a good move. I signed up for part-time evening shift work at the university hospital ER and full-time classes to get a Bachelor of Science in nursing (BSN). Nursing school curricula did not translate into much college credit, so I had to start with some freshman classes.

CHAPTER TEN

The Big City ER

My first impression of the university hospital was that everything looked *old!* I remember seeing wooden wheelchairs and stretchers that operated with cranks, like I had seen at the nursing home at the hospital where I had trained. Many of the stretchers also appeared in need of a trip to a car wash. A large desk sat in the corner of the waiting room. Behind and to the left of the desk there were automated double wooden doors that opened by pressing a silver disc on the wall. A nurse sat at the desk to triage patients, meaning she determined who needed to be seen by a doctor first. People were everywhere, and they were mostly black and poor. I was told approximately 300 people signed into the ER daily. The ER was their family doctor.

The nurse called multiple people to the desk at once. She asked each patient the reason for his or her visit and then popped a thermometer in each patient's mouth. I learned a new language. "Strain" was a common complaint, and it meant the patient had a discharge or symptoms of a sexually transmitted disease. "Fell out" meant passed out. Patients did not vomit, they "vomicked." One man told me he drank Clorox because he was crazy. He didn't smell of bleach, so I silently agreed he was crazy. A woman complained of fireballs in her "uckerus," which turned out to be fibroids in her uterus. She was having a problem with feminine bleeding. Someone gave a history of having "Smiling Mighty Jesus," which was spinal meningitis. If the patient did not appear to be in acute distress and had normal vital signs, that patient was told to take a seat, or else the patient was directed to an area called the Walk-in Clinic, which was open weekdays in the evening. It was like an urgent care facility today, but it was located at the hospital and was opened to alleviate some of the congestion from the ER. Residents were paid to work there during their free time.

There was a steady stream of ambulances. The antique intercom system we used announced, "Stretcher patient to be checked" as the patients were wheeled in. As each night I worked wore on, I noticed that the announcement did not elicit as quick a response as one would anticipate. We joked you had to be female in a tube top to get the prompt attention of the residents. Sometimes, the squad did not bring in the patient. The announcement in this case was, "A doctor is needed outside." This meant there was a body in the ambulance waiting to be pronounced dead. Sometimes, one of my coworkers got on the intercom and said, in a squeaky voice, "Help, help, let me out of this box!"

After a patient was seen by a nurse in the waiting room, the patient's chart was taken to the treatment area and placed in one of two wire baskets. One basket was for medical complaints and the other was for surgical complaints. The nurses tried to keep the patients in order until the time they registered, but they would reshuffle the patients whenever they assessed that a certain patient had more immediate needs than the other patients.

Patients were seen by the residents—the doctors who had graduated from medical school but were taking additional training for a specialty. The residents were supervised by a chief resident and someone called an *attending* who was an experienced practicing doctor. There were residents in many fields, and their training periods varied depending on their specialty. Orthopedics, internal medicine, family practice, and, of course, emergency medicine residents rotated monthly through the emergency department. There were some unbelievable days when I reported to work for my three P.M. shift and found the time on the top sheet in the basket was ten A.M. The residents were not speedy. Some of them also tried to pick through the pile to find a patient with a chief complaint that was appealing to them. If a nurse was in the vicinity she might slap the resident's hand and tell the resident to take the top sheet. Residents and nurses at the university hospital were on a more even footing.

A book called *House of God* came out about this time. It coined the word *gomer*, which stood for *get out of my emergency room*. Believe me, *gomer* was an apt term for the abusive drunks who did not bathe or use a toothbrush.

A gomer once came into the ER with a large gash in his face. He had been in the day before, and a plastic surgery resident had painstakingly stitched him up. Unfortunately, after he left the hospital, the man drank, got into a fight, fell, and basically undid the repair from the prior night. The doctor looked at him and decided to Steri-Strip him—that is, close the wound with simple paper tape.

It takes a special kind of person to maintain empathy. One night, a seasoned second-year resident came on duty, eyed the overflowing chart basket, and said, "Get me a prescription pad so I can get these gomers out of here." The absurdity of his statement lay in the fact that if a gomer had a dime, it usually went for liquor and cigarettes, certainly not to buy medication. We did try to send most gomers home with a little brown envelope containing a few pills to get them started. But I have no idea how many made any attempt to fill their prescription, or even how the welfare system worked at the time.

When a new shift started, the charge nurse from the departing shift walked around the entire department with a clipboard; she was followed by the incoming shift of nurses. She asked each patient his or her name and complaint and recorded this information on the clipboard, along with a notation of the patient's location. The clipboard would later be correlated with the charts in a rack at the desk in the waiting room. Each paper ER chart had a location handwritten in the corner that indicated the room the patient had been placed in him when he arrived. But the patient's location usually changed. They were moved to the hallway while waiting for lab studies and X-rays, which could take a few hours just because of the sheer number of patients. Patients also waited in the hallway for consults from another service. For example, a patient may have had a particularly high blood pressure reading, in which case the ER resident would have called the internal medicine resident for advice on the best medication to prescribe the patient.

One day while making rounds, we entered a room and found a patient dead. He had presented to the ER with a vague medical complaint and had apparently died before his chart hit the top of the basket. I was personally horrified. A resident was quickly summoned but there was no hoopla, no hysteria. No nothing. *Are they all numb?* I thought. *Will I become numb?* The man's body was sent to the coroner at the county morgue. Sadly, I knew that probably was the most luxurious digs the man had been in for a long time.

My memory of that time included the television show *Soul Train*, a black Dick Clark music-and-dance show. It seemed to be always on the TV in the ER waiting room. I had never known many black people, and I began to perceive they had a different frame of reference for life. They seemed to be able to express emotion more openly, both positively and negatively. They seemed to accept the endless hours of waiting to see a doctor without complaining. They seemed more family oriented than their white counterparts, and I admired them for this. If a grandma came in with a stroke, the waiting room would be full of visitors wanting to see her. White grandmas often seemed to be alone. During this time, I began to understand racial prejudice. A twenty-something white resident sauntered into the exam room with an older black man. This man, by the way, was polite and dignified; he was not a drunk. The resident said, in a condescending tone, "What's the problem, chief?" I could not imagine this type of tone being tolerated by someone like my father, a white professional engineer. It seemed like most doctors were white males who came from money. I thought that more than a few of them acted as if they were above certain other people.

As was the case where I had trained, the registration office typed exactly what each patient stated was the reason for the patient's ER visit. If the patient was unable to talk, the complaint was listed as a medical or surgical observation. One day, a patient who appeared to be a little old lady off the street was wheeled in, and she could not talk. The office was excited, though, because she had a purse—and, possibly, identification. The purse was empty except for a cockroach. It was so sad; all I could think was *Miss Cockroach from Cockroach Lane.*

It was also not unusual to see patients with maggots. This was extremely disgusting to me. It meant the patient had been incapacitated for a long period of time before someone had found the person and called the squad. We kept little brown bottles of ether in our main trauma rooms, and we poured the ether directly on the maggots to deep-six them. I never had a clue about the real reason to keep bottles of ether in the trauma rooms. Maggots can serve a noble purpose as far as wounds go, though: they consume dead tissue and can clean wounds. According to Wikipedia there are written records about their value in wounds dating back to the American Civil War and World War I. Again, I noticed (just as I had at my previous ER job) that probably two-thirds of all patient visits could have been handled in a doctor's office. People came to the ER with colds, coughs, cuts, sprains, and feminine complaints such as abnormal bleeding or a discharge possibly indicating infection. It was the other one-third of ER visits that challenged us.... that stoked our adrenaline and was the reason we worked in the ER. We were adrenaline junkies. Large inner-city hospitals received the catastrophic cases because they were teaching hospitals and there were always physicians available for all specialties onsite, around the clock. We saw unbelievable trauma, burns, complicated patients who needed surgery the suburban hospital could never have provided. As any given day progressed, the floors became littered with bits of gauze, drips of blood, and remnants of vomit. The sheer volume of patients made keeping the place clean a monumental challenge.

Christmas arrived. Prime overdose season. The holidays and the gloomy skies seemed to exacerbate depression. One evening, a twenty-something man arrived after overdosing. A family member intervened and called the squad. The man was lucid when he was admitted, so protocol called for us to give him ipecac and several glasses of water to induce vomiting. Our treatment worked, and he presented me with a pan containing a great deal of undigested spaghetti, in addition to the pills. I marched out of the room on my way to the hopper, holding the pan as far away from my face as possible while ignoring the mumblings of my patient (...hey, I'm human, too!) *Whoosh!* The offending contents were flushed away, just as the word *teeth* registered in my ears. When he had mumbled to me, the patient had been trying to tell me he had false teeth...

and I had just flushed them away. I made a futile call to the maintenance department. The man on the phone informed me, "Ma'am, they are in the sewer by now." I had to visit the psychiatrist who was on call, let him know about my mistake and ask for reimbursement for the patient. Lesson learned. Anyone can have false teeth, not just seniors, and I always asked after that. The toothless patient was able to go home in otherwise good shape.

Another overdose patient—a young woman—arrived by squad, but she barely roused with shouting and shaking. She was not a candidate for ipecac, so we inserted a large rubber tube through her nose and threaded it down into her stomach. We washed out her stomach with a couple of quarts of tap water. She was lucky; we saw visible pill fragments, so we had intervened in time. After she was thoroughly washed out (the medical term is *lavaged*), we instilled a black liquid, which was charcoal and water. We hoped this substance would absorb any residual medication that might have moved from the stomach and into her bowel before the lavage. The charcoal would cause her to take a big poop. When the patient awakened, she was angry. She shouted, "Goddamned socialistic medicine; you can't even take your life if you want to." I was totally dumbfounded.

Patients who overdose, and other psychiatric patients, often had long waits before they were admitted to the hospital because the beds on the psychiatric unit were usually full. If a patient was particularly unruly or disoriented as to time and place, we used leather hand restraints to attach the patient to the side rails of the stretcher. Then the patient was wheeled to the back hall of the ER to wait to be transferred. Patients weren't happy with this treatment;

they frequently shouted profanities at us as we walked by. Once, the most incredible thing happened: a huge man restrained to a stretcher was able to get himself standing upright while still attached to the stretcher. He was attempting to make a getaway, still attached to the stretcher. His strength was frightening: it took several security guards to get the situation under control.

One day, the intercom announced that a chaperone was needed in the back room. This was a frequent call throughout every shift. It meant a male resident was requesting a female attendant, so that the male resident could perform a gynecologic examination. This was a rule in the ER; it was put in place, so a male doctor couldn't be accused of misconduct. Also, if there was a need to check for infection during the examination, a nurse was always there to hand the instruments and swabs to the doctor. Once, when I was a little delayed getting to the gynecology room, the resident waved me away. He said a lady had been mopping the floor during his exam, and he considered her the chaperone.

The gynecology room had three wooden examination tables separated by curtains. Sometimes, women were brought there directly from jail and they were handcuffed to the examination tables by the police. It looked so inhuman to me, but, apparently, women used feminine complaints like lower abdominal pain or possible pregnancy problem as a ploy to get out of jail. The examination room for female patients was the last room in the long hallway of the ER. It was within feet of a door to a back hallway, which exited outside. Some unrestrained patients from jail had previously escaped unnoticed out the back door.

One night, a woman told the doctor she had a sponge stuck up inside her vagina. To his credit, the resident asked her, "Was that our mistake or yours?" Sometimes, things get overlooked in medicine; the resident was afraid someone had put packing in the patient after a vaginal operation and had not taken it out. The patient said it was her mistake. She had used a common household sponge instead of a tampon.

Sadly, we saw more than a few rape victims. We used a rape kit whenever we examined these patients; it contained bottles, bags, and tags. There was a strict protocol for handling the clothing and the swabs of bodily fluids. There was a documented "chain of evidence"—meaning we noted who received the evidence and when it was received. We were trained how to use the rape kit, but we were never really trained how to talk to the victim. We did, thankfully, have the phone number of a crisis center we could call. They always responded promptly.

Poor women reported to the city ER when they were in labor. For many, this was their first prenatal visit. The nurses put on gloves and did a vaginal examination to determine if the patient's cervix was dilated, a sign they were in labor. There was a chart on the wall with pictures of differently sized circles; each circle was labeled with a number from 1 to 10. The chart was meant to be used as a "cheat sheet" to describe what we were feeling during our examination, helping us estimate how dilated the patient's cervix was. If the cervix was dilated, we sent the patient upstairs to the obstetrical unit. If the patient's cervix did not feel dilated, the patient could be sent home, but our examination had to be confirmed by a physician.

A small-statured surgical resident once answered my call to check a patient. He had to stand on a footstool to perform the examination, because the patient was an extremely large woman. His hand and part of his arm seemed to be swallowed by her size. He was clearly uncomfortable in this capacity. He gave me a clueless look and said, "What did you get?" I silently asked myself: *Who is monitoring whom?*

The homeless and hungry regularly showed up at the ER. The experienced nurses and orderlies knew them by name. A man in ragged clothes was lying on a stretcher in the hall; a distraught resident hollered for a nurse. The resident was angry and nervous, thinking the man was in serious condition and had been overlooked by the nursing staff. As I was answering the call, I was passed by a coworker who had worked in the unit for many years. She stopped at the stretcher and said, "Archie, sit up for the doctor!" The man complied. He wasn't comatose, he just wanted some dinner. We didn't have much to offer, but we gave him some food. The hospital kitchen always sent brown bags of sandwiches, usually bologna and cheese, and cartons of fruit juice at the change of shift. Sometimes, we ate the sandwiches, too. The nurses took quick intermittent breaks in the utility room. We sat on round silver stools that ordinarily were used in the exam rooms (we used them to eat on or smoke a cigarette). We rarely left the unit for a real half-hour meal, because we were always short-staffed and didn't want to leave each other in a lurch. It was also a long walk to the cafeteria.

During one of our breaks, a sheepish resident walked into the utility room. He asked if one of us would give him a penicillin shot. He said he had gonorrhea. There was a microscope in the ER and some basic lab equipment, and the resident had diagnosed himself. We helped him out; it was all in a day's work.

The squad arrived with a flourish as they brought in the chauffeur of the state governor. He apparently had a heart attack on the job. After the hustle and bustle subsided, I overheard one of my coworkers, a nurse who had worked in the department for years, commenting: "Yeah, the *Gov* is out there, hanging over the desk, like all the other slobs." I didn't know what to say. Years later, I worked with a guy who had also worked in a big city hospital ER, and he commented, "Those ER nurses are so hard, they could eat their young!" I then remembered my coworker's statement about the governor and the slobs.

There were two sides to the ER—the adult side and the pediatric side. There were trained pediatric nurses, but when they were shorthanded the nurses in the adult side rotated over. One evening, I was asked to rotate to the pediatric area. I began helping with an asthmatic child. The resident gave me a verbal order to administer long-acting adrenaline, which was a medication we routinely gave in preparation for discharge. I administered the medication and walked out of the room to a visibly upset doctor. "Did you give it yet?" he asked. I said, "Yes." The doctor was shaken; he had ordered an adult dose, and I had given it. We had to call the chief resident down for a consultation. The child was admitted for cardiac monitoring overnight, because the side effect of the adrenaline was a racing heart. Blood pressure problems could develop, too. I was very upset. Thankfully, the child was able to tolerate the dose and made it through the night without any significant problems. I learned a huge lesson, namely, make certain the dose is correct. Everyone, even doctors, make mistakes—but not often, we hope.

On another night in the pediatric unit, a family rushed in screaming, "Her entrails are falling out!" The father was holding a young girl in his arms. We absolutely could not imagine what the father was screaming about. The girl had good color and did not appear to be bleeding. After we placed her in a room, the mother removed the girl's underpants...and there before our eyes was a large worm coming out of her rectum. This was a new one for me. I thought only animals got worms. But then, on second thought, we are mammals. *Hm*, I wondered. *Could some of our diseases be caused by worms...?*

We started another shift in a flurry. An auto accident victim was wheeled in while undergoing CPR. She was cold and looked grey. The chest compressions were briefly halted to see if the monitor displayed any electrical activity indicating the heart was beating. There were no signs of life. One of the nurses whipped her scissors from her pocket and cut down the entire front of the patient's clothes so we could better examine and work on her. Intravenous fluid was poured into her veins. One of the doctors placed a plastic tube down her throat to facilitate breathing. Another doctor asked for a tube to insert into her stomach. Suddenly, one of the seasoned nurses entered the room and piped out what many of us were thinking: "The woman is dead. Are you going to call her 'dead' or are you going to keep stuffing tubes in every orifice?" A resident retorted, "Your attitude is inappropriate, leave if you don't want to help." She left, and we continued, but everyone knew she had spoken the truth. After almost an hour, the familiar words were pronounced, "Call it," and the time of death was recorded.

I accepted a date with a doctor known as a "bad boy," and he picked me up in a Mercedes. We went to a party at the home of one of the social workers from the hospital. I soon found myself alone in the living room with one other guy I had never met. Everyone else, including my date, was in the next room smoking dope, popping pills...or popping something else. The lone guy in the room and I stood dipping chips and trying to make conversation. I had seen the effects of drugs on too many people and had decided the drug scene wasn't for me. I wasn't a goody-goody, I had tried marijuana, and it had made me dizzy and sick. Weird, since it's used as a drug by cancer patients, to treat their nausea. Maybe it was the smell; I really hated the smell of it.

On the way home that night, I lit a cigarette in the car. My date, the doper, went crazy. He said, "Don't smoke in my car!" I guess it was okay to smoke anything else, anywhere else, just not in his car.

We did not go out a second time. I was incredulous: professional doctors used illicit drugs?

Another resident asked me out, and this time we went to another doctor's house for a dinner party. Everyone seemed nice, no hippie drug nonsense, but after dinner the guys went to the living room to smoke pipes and discuss spinal taps. The women stayed in the kitchen, sharing their labor and delivery horror stories and their challenges with potty training. I felt out of place again, so I reported to the powder room to have a mini panic attack because this wasn't fun. I was twenty-four years old, and I guess I wasn't ready for marriage and motherhood.

Fortunately, a coworker befriended me. She had been an army nurse and was a Vietnam veteran. She introduced me to the local ski club, and that was the start of some fun times. No drugs, just lots of beer and poker on bus trips to ski destinations. The club regularly ran trips to Michigan, New York, and West Virginia for skiing. Before we departed from the designated parking lot, a plastic trash can was loaded onto the bus, filled to the brim with ice and beer. The tiny toilet in the back of the bus became quite atrocious.

Upper Michigan was my favorite place. I loved the crusty snow, the beautiful scenery, and the way I felt after a great day of exertion.

There was an outdoor pool at the resort lodge. It was heated and steaming, and I was goaded into bolting out of the building and taking a lap around the pool before jumping in with my friend, the ex-army nurse. She always had this thing about representing the women. She had to prove the girls could do a lap around the pool, in snow, in their swimsuits, just like the guys. After swimming and dinner, everyone went dancing at the lodge bar for a great time.

During the summer, the club rented houseboats for weekends on Lake Cumberland in Kentucky. They were our floating hotels. Some of the club members brought smaller motor boats to the lake so we could water ski. An equal number of guys and girls were assigned to each houseboat. On my first trip I learned the sleeping arrangements were dictated by what was called the "Law of the Lake." Everyone had to share a bed with someone of the opposite sex—and everyone complied. It was a dorm like situation in an open room, so nothing was really going on that I knew of.

On one of our trips my friend the army nurse was at it again. She talked me into jumping off (what I perceived to be) a high rock ledge with her, into the water of a cove. We would be representing the girls. Even though the rock ledge wasn't all that high; in retrospect, jumping off it probably wasn't the smartest idea, but we survived unscathed.

I learned the meaning of water conservation on these trips, because there was only so much water on the houseboat. We washed up in the lake with a bar of ivory soap. I also learned the meaning of a "lake enema." That was the term used when you crashed while water skiing and hit the water in just the wrong way!

Back at the hospital we experienced our first disaster, and it didn't involve a fire or a crash. It was the aftermath of a church supper. In the space of a few hours over twenty people arrived at the

ER with violent gastrointestinal illness—i.e., puking and diarrhea. We passed out metal pans to those patients who were vomiting but did not have enough bathrooms or stretchers. We had to ask some of the patients who were on stretchers to give them up and sit on a chair, so the more critically ill patients could lie down. Many of the church folks were elderly and had other preexisting medical problems. It was an exhausting night, and I heard "Lord Might Jesus" exclaimed a lot of times.

A young diabetic woman was a regular at the ER. Her diabetes was never controlled, or so it seemed. She was barely out of her teens, and she had been stuck for tests and intravenous fluids so frequently that it was difficult to find a vein. I found one in her thumb some nights, but other nights we had to give her cups of water to drink while we fiddled with her hands and arms looking for something to stick. One of the residents sat down and calculated that instead of paying for the patient's ER visits, the government that paid her bills (through welfare) could have rented a nice hotel room, provided a private duty nurse, and *still* saved money. We managed the woman's acute high blood sugar crisis but did nothing to prevent its reoccurrence. Today, case managers and diabetes educators are employed by hospitals and insurance companies to help patients with serious chronic conditions like diabetics, asthma, COPD and heart disease better manage their health. Computers identify these high-risk patients and then send the names and telephone numbers to nurses who will follow-up with a telephone call. I knew there were free clinics open for follow-up at the time, but a follow-up appointment at a clinic is of no use if the patient has no means of transportation.

It was a usual night in the ER, a chaotic mess. The baskets were piled with the charts of patients waiting to be seen. Suddenly, a resident came out of an examination room laughing. He pulled some of the nurses aside and quietly told us that the young guy he had just seen had a glass soda bottle up his rectum. He wasn't laughing so much about the soda bottle but about the fact that the patient had ridden his motorcycle in for treatment! The patient had to be brought to the operating room. I was never made privy as to how they got the bottle out. Then another guy came in a day or two later and said he had a pen in his bladder. He said it was in his mouth when he coughed and swallowed it. *That* was a better tale than the motorcycle man. I guess he didn't know the intestine was not connected to the bladder.

CHAPTER ELEVEN

Coronary Care

1975

I reconnected with a good friend from nursing school. She raved about a new hospital in the suburbs that paid exceptionally well; she was working there herself. She said they were well staffed and they had dinner breaks. When I went to apply I thought the grounds looked like a country club. The cafeteria had carpeting and floor-to-ceiling, draped windows overlooking a lush green lawn with trees. It looked like a fine restaurant. After working in a dirty and old building overlooking concrete, I did not need much convincing.

There weren't any openings in the ER when I applied, so I accepted a job in coronary care, on the evening shift. It turned out to be a good move. All the nurses in the unit were approximately the same age, and we were a harmonious team. We also socialized after hours or had lunches at each other's homes before our shift started.

The nurse's station had a master board of monitors that simultaneously displayed the heart rhythm of all the patients. We started each shift by printing a short paper strip recording of each patient's heart rhythm, it was like taking a small segment of an electrocardiogram. We Scotch-taped it in the nurse's notes section on the patient chart; we wrote our interpretation of the patient's heart rhythm underneath the strip. Because we watched cardiac monitors all day, every day, we became very good at detecting abnormalities with a single glance at the master board of monitors. We ran additional strips and added them to the patient's chart if we saw any new abnormalities. Correlating the information displayed on the monitor with that patient's condition is important. Certain heartbeat abnormalities are life threatening and need to be treated promptly. We had standing orders to administer certain drugs in emergency situations, without having to wait to reach a physician by phone or for them to arrive at the hospital. We could also administer electrical shock therapy, using paddles like you see on TV, again without waiting for a physician. I kept a spiral notebook of unusual EKG strips, creating my own mini-textbook. Since patients stayed for days, I got to know them in a more personal way than I ever did with patients in the ER. I enjoyed this aspect of the job.

Even at this stage in my career it was hard not to notice a difference in performance from one physician to another. All the nurses noticed that one doctor, who usually had the most patients on the floor, ordered the most narcotics. We also noticed that many of his patients had cardiograms and blood tests that were negative for a heart attack, yet the patients remained in the cardiac unit requesting narcotics around the clock. Several of us came right out with our concerns to the nursing supervisor. Nothing was ever said or done in response to our voiced concerns. It seemed that having a hospital operating at full capacity was more important than scrutinizing the quality of care the physicians were providing or ensuring the proper utilization of the cardiac unit.

So, the nurses protested in another way.

When Dr. Demerol (Demerol was the name of the favored narcotic) called in, some of us would make quacking noises in the background of the room, just loud enough for him to hear during the call. Was this sophomoric behavior? Yes, absolutely! But it was still a protest that was making an important point. Finally, one day Dr. Demerol was sighted rapidly walking down the hallway and writing orders for all his patients. He was changing the Demerol to a nonnarcotic alternative. Later, there were whispers that someone was finally looking over his shoulder, although we were not sure who that someone was. This change was short-lived, however; it was not long before he resumed his usual prescribing pattern.

There was another somewhat odd cardiologist who had a very thick European accent and was a chain smoker. He would leave a burning cigarette in an ashtray in the monitor room while he went to visit one of his patients. Then he would return, forget the first cigarette, and light another one. I overheard one my coworkers report a problem with a patient one day, and his reply was, "When you do too much, you do too much...a cardiac nurse should not be so nervous." He called someone "nervous"? What about his nervous cigarette habit? Yes, incredibly, people still smoked in the hospital in the mid-1970s. Even in the cardiac monitor room.

On each shift, the nurse in charge was called a team leader; at this hospital there was no official head nurse. I thought our team leader was excellent, and it was a good thing, because some of the house doctors did not fill us with confidence. Small private hospitals in the suburbs typically were not teaching hospitals, which meant there were no residents to call in an emergency. House doctors were hired by the hospital to fill in the gaps before the patients' doctors could arrive. There was a house doctor on every shift. They tended to be foreign; so, in addition to a language barrier, there was a cultural barrier, as many of the house doctors came from a culture that frowned on women working outside of the home, and they did not take suggestions from women very well.

One night, an elderly lady experienced a life-threatening condition: she had fluid in her lungs because her heart was not pumping adequately. Her diagnosis was congestive heart failure. The house doctor arrived after we paged him overhead, exclaiming, "STAT!" I entered the room and saw the team leader performing CPR on the patient and ordering medication while the house doctor sat in a chair and did nothing...except look at a *Reader's Digest* he had brought with him. I was directed by the team leader to go back to the station to call the patient's private doctor. He was a nice old man, but the nurses thought he was way past when he should have retired. He gave me what I thought was a very inappropriate medication order, and there was no reasoning with him. I knew that if the medication was administered to the patient, the patient might not be there in the morning. I debated whether to call the supervisor, but she was not a critical care nurse and would not have a frame of reference. She would call the medical director for the hospital, and the whole process could take an hour or two—time the patient did not have.

Fortunately, the old doctor had a son who also practiced at the hospital. I called him and told him about the patient and the order. There was a moment of dead silence and then he said, "Cancel his order, I'll be right in." Only then did I write the first order on the chart, followed by the second order to disregard it. Despite the mess that night, the little old lady made it—and she was ultimately discharged home. One of my coworkers saw her a month later at a local cafeteria enjoying a fried-chicken lunch, which is obviously not part of a heart healthy diet (or what we called a cardiac diet); still, it was a positive sign. You can't change human nature.

On another evening, I was talking with the team leader in one of the patient rooms. She was checking the patient's IV and preparing to give him some pills when he suddenly became unresponsive. On the cardiac monitor in the room, his heart rhythm was a fast, wide waveform moving across the screen.. Without missing a beat, the team leader clenched her right hand into a fist and gave the man a solid thump, right in the middle of his sternum. His heart rhythm returned to normal. This procedure is called a *precordial thump,* and it has fallen into disfavor over the years, but it was very effective this time. The man was then started on additional medication, per our standing protocol, to prevent reoccurrence of the abnormal heart rhythm.

Then I had my first "run-in" with a physician. My patient, a man in his sixties, had been admitted the previous night with a heart attack. I had done a double shift the day before and had admitted him myself during the night shift. I was back eight hours later for my usual evening shift and was assigned to him. He began having jaw pain that was not relieved by the narcotics that had been ordered. Then I noticed his blood pressure was lower than it had been at any time since his admission. I called his private doctor (also called the attending doctor) and reported my findings then received a short reply, something to the effect of "wait and see" and he seemed annoyed. Over the next hour the pain worsened, and so did the blood pressure. I placed a second call. This time I took the bold stance of asking the doctor if he was concerned about the blood pressure. By the tone of his voice I got the impression he was infuriated by being questioned by a twenty-something nurse. I got nowhere. He stated, "I don't wish to order anything at this time." My coworker placed the third call. I was at the patient's bedside with the house doctor, because the patient was in cardiac arrest. The house doctor ordered emergency drugs, and when the attending physician arrived they attempted to insert a pacemaker. The patient's heart did not respond, and I heard the familiar words again. "Call it."

Could the patient have been saved with earlier intervention? That was unclear. What was clear was the patient's physician seemed to have an ego problem and did not work well with the nurses. Later, when we were both completing our paperwork in the nurse's station the physician and I stared at each other, and he obviously knew I wasn't happy about the way the way he had talked with me on the phone and the patient's death. He said something to me like, "If you have a problem, make sure you approach it in the right way and very carefully."

I reported the incident to the nursing supervisor. Weeks passed. Finally, she called me into her office to inform me the case had been reviewed. An outside physician had seen the patient prior to his admission, and the physician had stated the patient had baseline disease that made him unsalvageable.

I said nothing. I did not rebut the physician's claim by arguing that I had admitted the patient myself and had taken his history. The patient told me he had no significant medical problems; I had recorded this. Patients are usually candid with nurses and sometimes tell them things they don't tell the doctor, so I found it hard to believe this patient lied to me. I remained angry about the case and the outcome for a long time.

Most of the nurses lined up in the tiny kitchen at about five P.M. to prepare the patients' dinners while one person watched the patients' heart rhythms on the master board in the nurse's station. The patients' food came in small packages, which we opened then placed on plates to put in the microwave. This was state-of-the-art at the time; patient food was delivered warm. It seemed silly to me to pay a registered nurse to microwave food, but we accepted this, just as we accepted other housekeeping tasks we had to do.

One evening, after delivering dinner, we had a horrendous thunderstorm. I looked outside the window in a patient's room, and I could have been looking through the round front window of a washing machine. The wind was howling. It was audible even inside the building; the television set warned of a tornado.

I became concerned. One of my coworkers passed me hurriedly in the hall, declaring, "I don't know about you, but I'm assuming crash position in the monitor room." I checked on my patients—they seemed not the least perturbed—before joining her. I pondered this later and realized the patients had survived the scare of coming into the emergency room with chest pain and then being given a diagnosis of damage to their heart. So, what was the big deal about a storm?

The new treatment protocol for patients who had experienced a heart attack included a new focus on diet. We restricted ice water (though I'm not sure why) and caffeine, and we put these patients on low-sodium diets. Most of the patients found the food on the low-sodium diet to be tasteless. It wasn't long before I noticed that some of them obtained saltine crackers. They scraped the salt off the crackers to salt their food. Now, why they just didn't tell the doctor the food was unpalatable is another story. The culture at the time was to never question the doctor. I must admit I didn't challenge the diet mantra, either; occasionally, I left some saltines at patients' bedsides.

No one addressed smoking, but it seemed that most patients were men and smokers. Many of the patients asked the doctor about resuming sex. The standing joke was, "Only with your wife."

Interestingly, the bathroom deal was a big issue with a physician when he became my patient. One day, we received a call from the ER saying that the thoracic surgeon, the guy who put in pace-makers for our patients, was there. We asked for the name of the patient—and they said *he* was the patient. We all looked at each other. There was a nonverbal consensus that everyone would be too intimidated to properly care for the surgeon. We decided to draw pencils to see who got him…and I lost.

The first thing the thoracic surgeon said to me after he was admitted to the unit was, "I want to be disconnected from the monitor to use the bathroom."

I disconnected him without saying a word.

The thoracic surgeon really was a nice man. At that time there was no such thing as a designated nurse in the radiology department who could assist with cardiac interventions. The coro-nary care nurse went to the department with the patient to watch the monitor and would set the external pacemaker. I had assisted the thoracic surgeon many times in the radiology department with pacemaker insertions.

Anyway, I overcame my intimidation of caring for the tho-racic surgeon after I listened to his chest for the first time. And as it turned out, he was in the coronary unit for only a few days. It was determined he had not had a heart attack, and his irregular heart rhythm was short-lived. His cardiologist attributed his symptoms to stress.

The assistant team leader had a baby. She reported that there was quite a production at her house the night of the delivery. Her water broke while her three-year-old was having a meltdown. She called her husband at work and the emergency squad. Her husband arrived at the same time the baby's head was appearing. She said her husband took one look and immediately started having an asthma attack. The squad delivered her baby at her home. She decided to take a little time off and then return part-time. I was offered the assistant team leader position, and I accepted.

My job as assistant team leader wasn't much different from my job as a staff nurse. I still took care of patients, but I was in charge whenever the team leader was off duty. I made the patient assignments for the shift and gave reports on all the patients to the nursing supervisor when she made her rounds. I also called the doctors, as necessary. I honestly do not recall if a pay raise was included in my promotion. If there was, I am sure it was minuscule.

An elderly patient came to the CCU from the floor with a very slow heart rate, something we called heart block. The patient had dementia and was unable to communicate meaningfully; instead, she made only sounds, mostly moans. She also was a bilateral leg amputee because of her diabetes, and she was constantly picking at the IV. So, we were fighting infection (probably a result of her constant picking) in addition to her failing heart. Her blood pressure was very low, and giving her medication for pain or sedation was problematic, because those drugs tend to lower blood pressure even more. She had no family. We had to restrain her to keep the IV in place.

Eventually, a cardiologist came in and decided to call the thoracic surgeon to insert a pacemaker. For the first time, the nurses really discussed what should be done or not done. There it was: *When do you preserve life? How long do you prolong death?*

All of us thought the patient should be left alone and kept comfortable. Someone said she wondered how the cardiologist would like dying while tied to the bedrails, just so an electronic device could be inserted in his chest wall to prolong his death.

One evening we received a patient from the emergency room with burns on his chest from the paddles used to deliver an electrical shock. He had received the electrical shock treatment while in the emergency room for an irregular heart rhythm, and he had been fully awake during the shock. The cardiologists usually delivered a lower voltage shock if the patient was awake and stable; they also usually sedated the patient prior to the procedure. I had no idea why this patient was burned, because the ER team was supposed to use a conduction jelly or pads to ensure the patient doesn't get burned. The patient made quite a fuss about his treatment in the ER; it went all the way to the CEO of the hospital. A few days later, a supervisor came to our department and asked to speak with me. She said the evening team leader in the ER was leaving, and that they were looking for a strong RN with cardiac experience to be the new team leader. She offered me the job.

CHAPTER TWELVE

Another ER

————◆————

I was excited to be back in the ER, but I was treated differently by my coworkers. I was their manager, yet I wanted to be everyone's friend. I had to learn the difference.

One of the nurses in the department was not particularly welcoming. I learned that she had expected to be offered the position.

So, maybe this goes without saying: my first few weeks were uncomfortable.

On one of my first evening shifts I was greeted by the news that a patient—a young man—had just died. He had arrived at the ER during the day shift, after suffering an accident on a construction site. He had been working on a local site, but he lived in another part of the state.

The patient's wife had been called and was on her way. She did not know her husband had died—we never tell people about a death on the telephone. The physician who had cared for the patient was now off duty; his replacement informed me he was not going to deal with the family. This left the task to me, since I was the nurse in charge.

It was a very painful start to a workday. Fortunately, I was able to reach the hospital chaplain, and he stood by me while I talked with the wife.

It was tragic; the couple had four young children.

One of the day shift nurses was particularly troubled by the case. She took me aside and told me that there had been a delay in reaching a surgeon to take the man to the operating room. She wondered if he could have been saved if he had been brought to the operating room sooner. We were a small suburban hospital, without the staffing resources of the inner city medical center. For all its failings, the inner city hospital is where you want to go if you are a victim of major trauma. When I worked there, a doctor from every specialty was always on the premises, and an anesthesiologist was always in the house.

My ski club nurse friend and I went on a rafting trip to West Virginia with a group of other hospital personnel. *I have no idea what I am in for,* I thought. Our guides gave us helmets, paddles, and brief instructions to plant our feet under the rounded edges of the raft before we took off. In the river, the raft acted like a bucking bronco. We went over a waterfall, which I swear looked like the one in the movie *How the West Was Won.* (If you're too young and missed the flick, the waterfall was HUGE.) No one fell out of the raft, and I felt a sense of accomplishment...but I would not do it again.

My work was somewhat like that waterfall.

The ER physician set the pace and the tone for our workday. Some were fast, some were slow, some were nice, some were arrogant. Some were career ER doctors; others were moonlighters—they didn't usually work in the ER but they were picking up extra money. Doctors who were finishing their specialty training and waiting to get their board certifications fit into this category. While working as the ER team leader, I had another confrontation with a physician. A patient arrived in medical distress, with low blood pressure and a heart rhythm that was very slow. A wide complex was displayed on the cardiac monitor. The ER doctor who was on duty was an orthopedic resident waiting to take his boards. He looked at the patient's heart rhythm and ordered medication. I had just finished a year on the cardiac unit and knew the medication was not correct for the heart rhythm, and I told him. I may not have spoken in the most diplomatic terms, but I basically told him "no," and that none of the nurses would administer the medication. The physician decided to retract the order and call for a consult with a cardiologist. Later, though, he angrily pulled me aside and told me he would speak to me again when I got my MD. And he never did speak to me again. He worked intermittently, and when he was on, he communicated with me through a coworker, even when I was in the same room. It was awkward, to say the least.

My ski club friend, the ex-army nurse, joined me at the suburban ER. A day shift position became available when she applied so she happily accepted it. She soon had her own work relationship problem. She was being pursued by a middle-aged, married man who worked in radiology. She was not interested and did not know how to address the situation, because her pursuer did not seem to want to take "no" for an answer.

My friend was doing some volunteer work, and I went with her one day to chaperone a group of kids to the local roller skating rink. So, who shows up but the guy from radiology? He proceeded to rent skates and wobble out onto the rink to impress my friend. He had overheard us talking about our plan to go to the rink. We had quite a laugh—and he still struck out.

A new physician was hired for the ER. He was arrogant and at times verbally abusive. One day when my friend was on duty and the designated nurse in charge for the day, a child came in with a serious case of croup. The child needed to be admitted so would have to be transferred to another hospital because our hospital provided ER care only for children. We had a specific procedure in place for this, but, instead of waiting for an ambulance, the problem physician called a police car. My friend argued with him to wait for the emergency medical squad, since the police were not trained emergency technicians or paramedics. He ignored her, and the child went out the door with the police. While she was still on duty that day, my friend was suspended for not preventing the transfer even though she protested. When I arrived for my shift, I could not believe she had been suspended! I was outraged! *Nothing,* apparently, had happened to the doctor who had caused the problem! It finally sent me over the edge, to the bathroom, to cry. Fortunately, a kind doctor was working on my shift that night. I didn't stay in the bathroom very long, but when I came out, he put his hand on my shoulder, looked at me, and said, "Something is really bothering you. Get back in there and finish your cry, you'll feel better."

The CEO of the hospital used to occasionally wander through the ER. One day, while I was charting, I felt fingers walking up my back, they were his. No words were spoken. A few days later, the problem MD worked my shift. He had a temper tantrum and threw a surgical instrument with a needle attached at one of my nurses. I filed a written complaint. Shortly thereafter, the problem physician was gone: fired by the CEO. I became known as the nurse who got him fired. I had never had any personal conversation or relationship with the CEO, but I'm glad he got rid of the bad guy.

I can't say it was the worst day of my career, but it was right up there.

It was spring, and we had a waiting room full of cuts, bumps, bruises, and sinus problems. All the patient rooms were full. It was almost eight P.M., and no one had taken a break, much less eaten dinner. Unbelievably, the nursing supervisor stopped by. After looking over the chaos, the supervisor commented that I didn't have my nursing hat on, and that, contrary to hospital policy, there was a Coke in the charting area. Just then, the squad called over the squawk box that they were bringing in a patient who was having a seizure. So, I was able to ignore the supervisor, for the time being.

When he was brought in, the patient had already been medicated by the squad, but his seizures had restarted, and he was still seizing when he arrived. His blood pressure was low, as well. We medicated him again and had just called for lab work when another squad called and said they were on their way with a victim from an automobile accident.

The victim was a lone driver, a teenage girl, and she had rear-ended a truck. She was unconscious and posturing: the muscles in her body had contracted, causing her arms and legs to assume a peculiar, extended, almost clenched position. Posturing like this occurs after a significant brain injury; the severity of the posture corresponds with the level of brain injury. The ER doctor had to immediately put a tube down the patient's throat, so she could be connected to a respirator. We administered medication intravenously, to decrease the swelling on her brain. (We treated symptoms without being able to visualize many details about the underlying problem; CAT scans hadn't been invented yet.)

Some of the staff stayed with the seizure patient, some stayed with the girl. Because I was the nurse in charge, I ran between the two rooms and tried to keep an eye on the rest of the patients. The hope was we would soon stabilize one of our critical patients and get that patient transferred to the ICU. Then, amid all the chaos, another patient, a man, stepped out into the hallway next to his room and just screamed at the top of his lungs. He had been waiting for someone to take care of him for over an hour, and, apparently, he had an insect in his ear. He could feel and hear it, he said. I felt for him (really, I did) but insects in ears are not life threatening. So, I had to ask him to go back to his room. Fortunately, both of our critical patients were stabilized and transferred to the ICU. About a week later, the same ER physician who had been on duty during the crazy night asked me to walk to the ICU with him, to see how the teenage girl was doing. She was still comatose, but while we were standing at her bedside she moved one of her arms upward, bending it at the elbow. The physician was excited. "Did you see that?" he said to me. "That was a good movement; it means the swelling in her brain is decreasing." The ER doctor had been a neurologist in a previous life. He had come to America, escaping political upheaval in his country. Nothing else was ever shared between us. He was simply working in the emergency room until all his credentials were processed.

One of the most unusual cases I ever saw was brought in by the squad from a tiny outlying hospital. The patient was a young woman who was comatose and had dried, bloody bandages over both of her wrists. The squad said she was found with slashed wrists, in a bathtub of blood, after apparently attempting suicide. She had received blood at the first hospital. Her monitor showed a slow irregular heart rhythm, but her blood pressure was acceptable. We drew labs; her hemoglobin level was 20, which was way above normal. Maybe, we thought, she hadn't bled significantly and had incorrectly been given the blood? So...why was she comatose? The ER doctor said she had probably taken an overdose. He was right: she responded well once we supported her breathing efforts and administered an antidote for narcotics intravenously. After a stay in the ICU she fully recovered and was referred for mental health therapy.

Another unusual case involved a ten-year-old girl. She was brought in by the squad from home. Her speech and behavior could be described only as bizarre. Our first thought was she might have ingested drugs, but her parents assured us she had never been in any trouble, and that she had never behaved like she was behaving today. We then thought there might be some psychiatric problem, because her preliminary vital signs were normal. When we were told she had recently recovered from the measles, she was admitted. It was determined with a lab test of the spinal fluid that she had measles-induced encephalitis, a rare complication caused by inflammation in the brain. The girl eventually made a full recovery, and I learned the importance of obtaining a thorough history.

There were several other awkward issues I encountered while I was on the job. Some of the foreign-born moonlighters had different hygienic habits than what we were used to. The doctors and nurses shared a very small area in which they completed their documentation, and one young man had a very significant B.O. problem. The nurses decided someone had to talk with him. We drew pencils. Fortunately, this time, I was not the loser.

Another time, a group of us were sitting in the cafeteria, eating dinner. I couldn't believe my eyes when I saw the ER doctor pick up the salt shaker and coat his spaghetti. Then, after we had finished eating, the unit clerk lit a cigarette. The ER doctor jumped at the opportunity to lecture her on the danger of cigarettes. She looked at his plate and said, "Tell you what, I'll keep my cigarettes and you keep your salt shaker and we'll see who dies first."

CHAPTER THIRTEEN

ICU

———————◆———————

1977

The ER nurse decided to try intensive care nursing. I had a boy-friend now, and three years working the evening shift was long enough. I wanted a day shift job again.

Fortunately, right around this time, an assistant director of nursing at another hospital joined my tennis league. When she found out I was a critical care nurse, she told me the hospital's ICU had open day positions that included a night rotation. The rotation entailed four weeks on day shift followed by two weeks on night shift. She encouraged me to check out the hospital and assured me that critical care nurses were "gold in the bank" there. I took her advice…and I was offered one of the positions. It included a pay raise, even though I would be stepping down from a managerial position to be a staff nurse again.

The patient care unit was one large room with three smaller private patient rooms off to one side. A unit clerk sat in a small room next to the patient care area and answered phone calls and processed doctor's orders by filling out laboratory and X-ray request slips. The charts were kept in her room. The head nurse also had an office. There was a quiet room, too, which was used for the life-altering conversations with families; it was also used for staff meetings.

The large room was divided in half by a shoulder-high wall; it accommodated up to eighteen patients. The ICU beds were bigger than an ER stretcher but smaller than a regular hospital bed. A cardiac monitor was mounted at the head of all beds. Each bed was also surrounded by curtains on tracks mounted on the ceiling; the curtains could serve as a privacy shield. Visiting hours were very limited.

At one end of the room there was a long counter with two phones and medical reference books. The master cardiac monitoring system for all the patients was mounted on the wall above the counter. You could follow the bouncing blips with your eyes. It made me think of childhood cartoons that showed a ball bouncing over the words to a song. A glass window in the wall next to the monitors allowed a view of the chart room where the unit clerk sat. The window slid open just like at a fast-food place; it allowed the nurses and the secretary to pass charts back and forth. The end of the room that was opposite the monitors opened onto a small kitchen, utility room, and a back hall, which had a nurse's lounge.

There were no outside windows in the unit, and the patients sometimes developed what we called ICU psychosis, because they had no sense of day or night. The sights, sounds, and smells were very striking in the patient care area. Most patients were hooked up to multiple machines and had several intravenous drips that operated on control pumps. Lights in the pumps blinked as the medication was being delivered, and alarms on the pumps would be set off if the IV tubing got kinked or the IV bag was empty. The respirators made a humming noise, and there was a jarring alarm whenever the tubing became disconnected. The nurses regularly disconnected the tubing to suction mucous out of the patient's breathing passages. Patients sometimes just coughed the tubing apart too. But it was hospital policy to never turn off the alarms, so no one would forget to turn them back on.

The heart monitors also had alarms, and they went off more frequently than the alarms on the respirators. The machines couldn't always distinguish a heart rhythm that was truly abnormal from a momentary change in rhythm caused by the patient moving around in bed. We had to frequently silence the heart monitor alarms with a reset button.

Patients who had open heart surgery or lung surgery had plastic tubes in their chest walls for drainage. The tubes were attached to a sealed suction device that made a gurgling sound, kind of like the sound made by an electric filter in a home aquarium. I thought I was in a science fiction movie when I first started working at the unit.

I still remember the smells of the unit, too. We administered a special IV fluid to meet the nutritional needs of patients who were unable to eat for a prolonged period. It was a mixture of sugar, salt, and minerals, and it had a sickeningly sweet smell.

Antibiotics had their own peculiar odor; many reminded me of the smell of decomposing lawn clippings. The nurses prepared all the antibiotic drips for the patients, and they often inadvertently sprayed a little of the IV fluid on their hands while expelling the air out of the syringe before injecting the drug into the intravenous bags. Sometimes there was an odor of urine, because many of the patients had catheters, which drained their urine into bags; the bags had to be emptied regularly. In the morning, there was a mixture of odors from bedpans and bath soap. Breakfast trays with tea or broth also scented the room, though only a few patients were well enough to eat on any given day. Once, when I was at my boyfriend's office, I was struck by the quiet. The only thing I smelled was new carpet and coffee. I had not realized the constant environmental stimulation we were subjected to in the ICU, and that we had somehow learned to filter it out.

When we arrived for our shift, we checked the assignment sheet at the front counter. We usually had two patients; but it was possible to have three if someone called in sick or the unit was completely full. Patients who needed constant intervention, such as someone who had just come out of the operating room after open-heart surgery, would have a dedicated nurse assigned only to them. Constant intervention meant the patient was on a respirator, needed his or her vital signs taken and recorded hourly, and was on IV drips that profoundly affected the patient's circulatory system and required strict monitoring.

The bedside table that raised, lowered, and fit over a patient's bed to hold a food tray was kept at the foot of the bed and used for supplies and a writing desk for the nurse. Nurses sat on small armless chairs with wheels at the bedside table during the change of shift. The departing nurses gave a verbal report about their patients to the nurses who were coming on duty and now assigned to the patients. The only nurse who received a full unit report on ever patient was the charge nurse. Report included the history, most recent lab values, X-ray reports, medications, and the patient's progress in general. We also shared some personal talk and had a cup of coffee. Since we rotated shifts, there wasn't much nit-picking about what had or hadn't been done on the previous shift, as I had noticed at my previous job.

Most of us were in our twenties, and we were about evenly split regarding whether we were married or unmarried. I was in the "unmarried" category, having parted with my longtime high school boyfriend, who was the only boyfriend I had ever contemplated being married to. The unmarried nurses awaited the new crop of residents every year. I never figured out who got the information on the marital status of the new residents, but it was available almost immediately after they arrived and circulated widely.

The residents and the nurses generally had a good working relationship. Many new residents were "book" smart but not totally comfortable regarding the practical applications of what they had learned. They asked the nurses for their opinion. They knew we had honed our observation skills. We looked, felt, smelled, and listened...and then we told them what we thought. Unfortunately, a few older attending physicians still had an ego problem. It was a shame that these physicians wouldn't dream of asking for our input. We were always very careful to phrase suggestions to these doctors regarding treatments or medications with, "Some of the other doctors have tried…." We could never come right out and say, "I think the patient needs to have some additional pain medication," or, "In my opinion, the patient is ready to try some clear liquids."

Once, I found my coworker having a heated disagreement with a consulting specialist. The specialist had ordered a tube to be inserted down the nose of a young girl to check for a gastrointestinal bleed in her stomach. The girl was retarded and deaf, and she had a normal pulse and blood pressure, so she did not seem to be in immediate danger. My coworker asked the doctor to wait for the child's interpreter to tell the child what we planned to do so she would not be frightened and fight us. The doctor was impatient and wanted it done immediately. They took their fight to the back hall. My coworker won this one for the patient; occasionally, we do.

After the nurses completed their reports, the nurses starting their shift performed a total body assessment of the patient. I started with my patient's hands for two reasons. First, I believe touch says, "I care." And I *did* care. I was also looking at the fingernails to assess the patient's respiratory status. I looked at the color and the shape of the nail beds. Blue nails were obviously not good, and clubbed nails indicated the patient had chronic respiratory disease. After examining the patient's hands, I always took a quick look at the patient's feet while feeling for pulses. This gave me a good idea of the overall status of the patient's circulatory system. Feet should be warm and have good color. Pulses should be easily detected on the top of the foot and by the ankle. I paid attention to the patient's speech and determined whether they were alert and oriented to time and place. Some patients can be awake but have no idea what day of the week or year it is, and no idea of where they are. Next, I took the patient's vital signs and listened to their breathing and bowel sounds. I recorded all my findings.

All human beings need touch. That is what nursing care is for and about. It might mean holding a hand, feeding a patient an ice cube, or just frequent repositioning of a limb to provide comfort. One outstanding coworker told me she practiced positioning herself with pillows in her bed at home, so she would know what positions were comfortable for her patients. Maintaining IV lines and assistive machines are not the only important parts of the job. About every two hours, we allowed visitors into the unit for a short period of time, usually fewer than fifteen minutes. They bolted in when the clerk announced it was visiting time. They were frightened and often tired. Many often had spent the previous night on the vinyl sofas in the waiting area so they could be near the patient in case there was an unexpected change for the worse.

The patient care routine for the shift was: assessment, vital signs, administration of medications (as scheduled), administration of pulmonary care (if the patient was on a respirator), administration of wound care (as needed), and repositioning of the patient at regular intervals (so they would not get bedsores). We scrutinized lab reports as soon as we received them, and we called the doctor to discuss any abnormalities. In between all of this, we communicated the patient's status to his or her family and tried to soothe their fears and pain.

I was climbing the steep hill from the hospital garage for my night shift. It was a summer night, and incredibly hot and humid. I was so very tired. Even though I had been in bed for over nine hours, I had been awakened repeatedly, and I did not feel well rested. I had room-darkening shades, and I had unplugged the phone—but you can't stop the kid next door from bouncing a basketball, or the toddler making *click-clack* noises with a toy in his driveway. I would need to hit the coffee pot as soon as I arrived at the unit.

It was a routine night...until I encountered a serious glitch. I prepared and hung an IV medication, then connected it into the IV that was already running through a rubber port on the tubing. As soon as the medication hit the existing drip, the liquid precipitated. It looked like milk. This was very bad and jolted me into action. I had to turn off the whole IV system and prepare a new line. I swapped the two lines at the IV insertion site, which takes some practice to do. No coffee was needed at that moment; I was wide awake. Today, pharmacies prepare most IV drips and remind the nurses about precipitation risks in which case the patient might need a separate intravenous line.Coffee kept me going until about five A.M. Then I splashed cold water on my face, paced around the floor...anything to make it through the final two hours of my shift. If I revisited the coffee pot, I would have had trouble falling asleep when I got home, even though I would be completely exhausted.

On my next night shift, one of my patients was an organ donor. His car had been hit by a train; he had been declared brain-dead. He was a young man. We were keeping him alive with a respirator and by running IV fluid to keep his kidneys functioning until it could be determined whether he matched someone on a kidney transplant waiting list. His face had been horribly "smashed" in the accident; the nurses kept a bath towel across the upper part of his face, leaving only his mouth and the respirator tube uncovered so they could access them. But the towel was also for our benefit, our comfort, so we did not have to continually look at him. Unexpectedly, the clerk told me there was a woman in the waiting room who wanted to see the patient, and she claimed to be his fiancée. No one claiming to be a fiancée had visited before. We always kept a notation about significant others on the chart. When I was able to, I went to speak with the woman. I was surprised to see she looked old enough to be his mother.

She had dirty straggly hair, was wearing a pair of knit shorts, and had a catheter (a drainage tube for urine) snaking out of the bottom of her shorts until it disappeared into a shopping bag. (The tubing ended in a plastic bag inside the shopping bag.) She smelled of alcohol and appeared to be drunk, and she demanded to speak with the doctor. I had no idea what she knew or didn't know about my patient's condition. It was peculiar: the patient had been here for a few days, but this was the fiancée's first appearance. I called the resident, and we went into a small room, the head nurse's office, so I could tell him about the visitor. I was very tired, and I proceeded to have an inappropriate meltdown as I tried to explain the situation and the reason I had called him. The sight of the poor victim was horrendous enough, and now there was a disheveled drunk woman with a catheter in a shopping bag demanding patient information. I broke into laughter at the absurdity of reality. The resident was also tired. He looked at me and began laughing, too. We closed the door because we couldn't stop laughing. I said "okay, okay" and smacked myself on the side of my face to straighten up. But it was futile. I kept laughing.

We were in there for quite some time before we were able to compose ourselves and call in the woman.

My recollection ends there. I assume the man donated his body parts, according to plan.

One of the nurses who worked at our hospital was also involved in a tragic car accident. She was on a medical floor, so I did not know her personally. Her car went off the road during a storm and crashed into a tree. She arrived in a comatose state and never woke up. Over the course of the next few weeks, all neurologic tests indicated she had irreversible brain death. The family made the decision to remove her respirator even though she was in her twenties. It was done quietly, with the family and the neurosurgeon in attendance. There were no protesters or threatened lawsuits. I know that, today, some people would call this euthanasia and claim that it was immoral. I honestly never thought of it that way. I would want the same thing for myself, if I were ever in her position.

It was once again the nurse's job to wrap the body in the plastic sheeting and load it on the stretcher with the hidden compartment for transport. Death is so very sad when the person is so young. I accepted death so much better when the patient was elderly and I could assume had at least tasted life.

We were busy that day, as usual, and I had little time to grieve. I filed the experience away in my head for another time.

Often during my career I have asked myself if our life span is pre-ordained. If the answer to that question is "yes," it would offer one explanation for why patients who have physiological markers that point to certain death survive against all odds.

A middle-aged man entered our unit with inflammation of his pancreas, a complication of a bad gallbladder. The inflammation had progressed to an overwhelming infection, and his kidneys had shut down. We had to put him on a respirator, and he had to be dialyzed. To maintain a high enough blood pressure to sustain his life, he was placed on the maximum dose of an IV medication. The downside of the medication was that it constricted the small blood vessels in the patient's extremities; his distal limbs began darkening. It looked like frostbite, but this was chemically induced. He was intermittently conscious and, overall, a tragic sight. His life was hanging by a thread.

Numerous consulting physicians reviewed the patient's chart in the doorway; they maybe spent a minute or two at his bedside. Most did not lay a hand on him. Since his vital signs and laboratory values indicated death was imminent, they seemed to not want to deal with it. When one "doorway" clinician asked the assigned nurse how the patient was doing, she replied, in exasperation, "JP FROG." *Just Plain Fucking Run Out of Gas.* The physician did not respond and, instead, made a hasty retreat. Miraculously, the man survived. Ultimately, he even made it out of the hospital.

Later, whenever I looked back on that patient, I always felt that it just wasn't his time.

It was seven A.M. on April Fool's Day, and after checking the assignment sheet I walked to one of my assigned patient's bedside to wait for the departing night shift nurse to give me report on their condition. There was a ruckus outside one of the private rooms, so I veered off to see what was going on.

If a patient was in a private room, it meant they had a significant infection that needed to be treated in isolation or, possibly, that they were a renal patient and needed dialysis. There were drains in the floor of all the private rooms. The patient chart said this patient was on a respirator. Our usual respirators were about the size of a dishwasher. There was a bellows encased in a plastic cylinder on the top of this machine. Control dials sat next to it. I noticed the patient was in a large cylindrical tube; just her head was visible. She was wearing a hat like a paper shower cap. Multiple IV tubes dangled above the cylindrical tube and disappeared into it. I was totally clueless about the equipment until the night nurse informed everyone it was an iron lung. It was being used on the patient (she said) because we had run out of respirators. The chart said the patient's name was "Annie Ironsides" and that she was allergic to heavy metals.

Even in the dim light we soon realized something was not quite right about the patient. Her chest rose and fell with the respirator, but her limbs were a little too straight and stiff. Upon closer inspection, the "patient" turned out to be the vinyl demo doll we used for CPR class. I laughed with the rest of the nurses who had crowded around Annie (the name everyone used for the doll). It must have taken a real team effort to get that iron lung up to the unit, and it provided a welcome moment of hilarity amid so much suffering and death. Downtime and low census (empty beds in the unit) were rarities, but we knew how to make the best of them.

The best comic show involved a horse—or, at least, a rendition of one. According to news reports, several horses had died during the night in a fire at a local stable. Some of the horses were reputed to have been potential racing champions. I arrived at the unit for my morning shift and followed the crowd to a mound spread across two hospital beds that were pushed together. The mound was covered with blankets, and they appeared to be in the shape of a horse. A banner hanging from the ceiling proclaimed: "He was a Hell of a Horse." A chart on the bedside table named the horse "Flicka." Dr. Appaloosa was listed as the horse's physician. Flicka was of course allergic to *haycillin*. The best part of this foolishness was the quizzical looks from the physicians walking in for their morning rounds. One surgeon who was well known for his ill humor walked to the bedside and lifted a corner of the blankets. Then, he cracked a smile.

We received a young man who had been involved in some sort of brawl and had multiple fractures and lacerations. He was in the unit for observation, to rule out internal bleeding, but he was expected to transfer within a day or so and then make a full recovery. And that was a good thing, because he had not one but three women in the waiting room. They each claimed to be his significant other. There was a wife, an ex-wife, and a girlfriend. I don't recall him looking like anything out of Hollywood. And I *do* recall one of my coworkers checking under his covers.

We soon had another young man of note. He was in our unit for observation for a head injury after being beaned repeatedly with a rock. He also had a very badly torn ear. When we learned the details, it was hard to muster sympathy for him. He had taken two teenage girls at gunpoint to a deserted spot. The girls were apparently very frightened and didn't attempt to resist. He was in the process of raping one of them when the other picked up a large rock and slammed it into his head. The other bit his ear. They then proceeded to beat him. Supposedly, one of the girls picked up the gun and fully intended to shoot him but didn't know how to make the gun work, and it didn't go off. I heard the story from the neurologist on the case. He probably got his information from a chatty ER staff member. It was an incredible story. I guess we don't know what we are capable of when we're threatened.

The neurologist then checked on another patient he had in the unit, and his expression became one that seemed both sad and perplexed. The patient—a woman around forty years old—had had a small tumor excised from her brain. She was awake but not communicating and not following commands. The neurosurgeon who had performed the surgery was looking for an explanation for this outcome. He explained that the amount of tissue he had removed was very small.

One of the hospital's claims to fame was its expertise in cardio-thoracic surgery. We performed over two hundred open-heart operations a year. The nurses in the ICU were given the names of patients scheduled for open-heart surgery the day before their surgery. The nurse assigned to an open-heart surgery operation visited the patient the afternoon before the day of surgery to provide pre-op information. The patient was told that they would wake up from anesthesia with a tube in their throat, and that they would be breathing with the aid of a respirator. They would not be able to speak. The tube would be removed as quickly as possible; they should not panic or struggle with the breathing tube. We assured them someone would be watching them constantly, and that their pain would be well managed.

Today, insurance companies no longer pay for patients' overnight stay before the operation, so patients do not meet the nurse who will care for them beforehand. Today, patients typically report for a pre-op outpatient assessment at the hospital a few weeks before their operation. During the outpatient assessment, they have appropriate blood work done, and X-rays are taken for their operation. It is up to the physician and his office staff to prepare patients for what to expect when they wake up from surgery. The old personal touch is gone.

After the operation was complete, the heart patients were brought directly from the operating table to the ICU; there was no stop in a recovery room in between. The nurses prepared the area around the patient's bed before the patient arrived by setting up a mercury manometer that would be connected to a saline line, which in turn would be inserted into an artery in the patient's arm. The line continually measured the patient's blood pressure; we also used the line to withdraw blood for lab tests. Mercury had not yet been declared a serious toxin; sometimes, when we were setting up the manometer, some of it would spill on the bedside table, where it would collect in a silver puddle. We would scoop it up with paper and place it back in a plastic cup without a second thought.

A mercury manometer is unheard of today. Instead, the IV line is now attached to a small electronic machine that provides a continuous waveform and a digital readout of the patient's blood pressure on a monitor mounted above the bed. During the immediate post-op period for patients who have undergone an open-heart operation, vital signs are monitored and recorded hourly. We also monitored the amount of drainage coming out of the chest tubes that had been inserted into the patient. These tubes were stitched into the chest wall during surgery. When I was new, I watched one of the seasoned nurses give her new postoperative heart surgery patient a complete look over. She then turned to the cardiothoracic surgeon and said, "I want the phone number where you will be, I have a feeling this one might be a return." She didn't like the amount of drainage coming out of the chest tubes. The surgeon complied, as he respected her opinion.

A patient's blood potassium levels are often low after surgery, so lab work is performed to check the level every couple of hours during the immediate post-op period. Potassium was replaced intravenously, as needed. If the heart monitor showed an irregular heartbeat, we typically started a second IV in another site to give the patient drugs to soothe their heart muscle. These IV drips would be controlled by a pump to ensure the dosage was delivered accurately. Pain medications were also delivered through the IV line. We used a board that had the alphabet on it; the patients could communicate by pointing to letters to form a word. By the second day after a heart bypass, patients were usually off their respirator and sitting up, sipping clear liquids. Overwhelmingly, patients had a good outcome. They transferred out of the ICU to the step-down unit by day three.

As one of my coworkers and I sat down with our trays to eat in the cafeteria, my coworker noticed something strange on her left hand. Her wedding ring was no longer gold in color, but silver. She was the nurse assigned to the open-heart surgery patient that day, and she had already set up the mercury manometer. Did the color of her ring have something to do with the mercury? We frequently experienced chapped hands from the iodine soap we used; sometimes they even bled. But we had never seen a wedding ring change color.

I began to wonder about a run of miscarriages among the nurses in our unit, and whether it could be connected to "stuff" we were exposed to daily. Within the past two years, three nurses had miscarried. Another had suffered a fetal death, just before delivery. The number of miscarriages seemed high, but no one ever considered it or kept a record that I knew of. I particularly wondered about all the medications we handled. At that time, nurses prepared essentially all medications that were administered intravenously. We washed our hands but did not routinely wear gloves when preparing the medication. It was customary to expel air bubbles from syringes after drawing up a medication—and it wasn't unusual for some of the fine spray to get on your hands while doing this. Today, hospital pharmacists wearing gloves prepare most IV medications in the pharmacy. This is good for the patients, because theoretically the pharmacy is a lot cleaner than the ICU. (The source of germs in the ICU is the patients themselves!) Every little step to ensure cleanliness helps to reduce the incidence of hospital-acquired infection. I think it is also good for the nurses, because it reduces exposure to medication.

She came to our unit, rushed from labor and delivery, and became another incredible story. She had developed severe difficulty breathing immediately after the delivery of her baby. The doctors had to insert a tube through her mouth and connect her to a respirator. She thrashed about the bed, and her eyes were filled with fright. Even with the respirator, she was not getting enough oxygen. Her condition was critical. She was my age....I was frightened for her.

There were several doctors at her bedside, and they seemed uneasy. This was an unusual case: they thought she had thrown a clot to her lung. They sedated her and cranked up the respirator.

Then we could no longer hear her breathing on one side of her chest. One of her lungs had collapsed, which was sometimes an unavoidable side-effect of the high setting of the respirator. A chest tube now had to be inserted to allow the collapsed lung could inflate.

We gave her a paralytic drug and simultaneously sedated her to better control her ventilation. Days passed. Then a week. The nurses lubricated her eyes and kept little pieces of plastic over her eyelids to keep them closed because she was unable to blink. We turned her at least every two hours so she would not develop a pressure sore. We kept the rubber tube to her bladder clean. She was a nursing triumph: she never developed a urinary tract infection, skin breakdown, or a problem with her eyes. Nursing care was provided to her as it was supposed to be.

Her chest tube was finally taken out. We reduced her medication, and we were finally weaning her from the respirator when there was another setback.

At approximately five A.M., I was sitting at her bedside, propping up my head with my hands, fighting my urge to doze. I glanced at her—and suddenly I noticed her lip color looked bluish. No alarms had gone off; she was still on the respirator. But I was alarmed at her appearance.

I jumped up and listened to her breathing with my stethoscope, then called the resident. She had *another* collapsed lung. A chest tube had to be inserted again; it would be another week before we could finally remove the tube and wean her off the respirator. After she was breathing on her own, and before she transferred to the step-down unit, she told one of the nurses that she had still been awake and aware during some of the time that she was "paralyzed and sedated." She said she did crossword puzzles in her head to keep from going crazy.

Months later, a woman came up to me in the grocery store. She said, "You were one of my ICU nurses, I'm C—." She was smiling, and there was a healthy baby in her cart. It was the most incredible, "feel-good" encounter I had had as a nurse.

It was a very bad night.

A patient went into cardiac arrest and there was a prolonged resuscitation effort. Even though a resuscitation is easier to per-form on an ICU patient than on an ER patient (because an IV is in place, and baseline laboratory test results are available), it is still an emotional event.

We no sooner had resolved the first crisis when a second patient went into arrest. Her name was Lucille, and the nurse assigned to her was softly singing words to the country tune "Lucille," crooning "You picked a fine time to leave me, Lucille" as she wheeled the red metal crash cart to the second patient's bed-side. I admired the nurse's calm; I was finding caring for these crit-ical situations a psychological drain: I needed a break.

A break finally came in the form of an adorable four-year-old boy. He had been in the unit, in a croup tent, for almost two days. Croup is a viral respiratory infection that causes inflammation and a narrowing of the respiratory passageways, making breath-ing difficult. A croup tent was used to deliver a humidified mist that helped to reduce inflammation. The boy had been sedated, and the doctors had reduced his sedation level on the previous shift, because the readings of his oxygen levels had improved. He awakened on my night shift and demanded his mama and his underpants. He was going to be alright.

On the night shift, we frequently did not have enough staff to take our half-hour dinner break out of the department. We took turns going to the cafeteria and brought our food back upstairs to eat at our patient's bedside table. No one thought to complain, it was part of the job. We also took turns being the nurse in charge on evening and night shifts. The head nurse designated who was to be in charge by noting it on the assignment sheet posted in the front of the room. There was no additional pay for the honor, and the charge nurses on the off shifts still took care of patients.

We had a problem nurse who constantly called in sick or late. When she gave her notice, we were all relieved, because it was always a burden when someone called off her shift. Before her last scheduled night, we started a betting pool, and everyone put some money in a jar. Would she show up on her last night? If so, how late would she be for her shift?

She did show...but she was *very* late.

One day, nursing care was not provided as it should have been and staffing most assuredly played a part.

We had a patient recovering from Guillain-Barré syndrome, a rare disorder in which the body's immune system attacks the nerves. The patient was on a respirator, but her vital signs were stable, and she communicated with the nurses using the letter board, until one day when her cardiac monitor suddenly rang off. Her heart was in full arrest. When the nurses got to her bedside, they found she was disconnected from her respirator and the alarm on the respirator had been turned off. Alarms were *never* supposed to be turned off. Patients sometimes coughed the respirator tubing off, but they were always promptly attended to because of the loud alarm. In this case, it was possible the lack of oxygen had caused the cardiac arrest. After the incident, her mental status never fully returned while she was still in the unit. I never heard about her long-term outcome after she transferred out.

I was not on duty the day that incident happened; I was told this story by another nurse. The incident occurred during lunch-time, and two nurses were watching one half of the room with seven patients. One of the two nurses "minding" the seven patients was on the phone with a doctor in the front of the room and the other was fully garbed and in a private room with an isolation patient. No one noticed the respirator was off the patient until the alarm on her heart monitor went off.

My two intensive care patients were stable and ready to transfer, so the charge nurse told me I had to take the new admission from the floor. The patient was a middle-aged man apparently septic—infection had overwhelmed his body, and his blood pressure was dangerously low. The step-down unit nurse who assisted with his transfer said he was post-op coronary bypass surgery the previous week and had been in our unit. I had not cared for him after his surgery, so I was not familiar with his history. Currently his temperature was over 104ºF, and the site on his leg where they took the vein for the bypass grafts was inflamed and seeping. Samples from his leg had been cultured a few days prior, and he was on antibiotics. He was also a diabetic, which can predispose people to infection.

I took the report from the step-down floor nurse and hooked the man up to our equipment. Then I looked through the results of all his latest laboratory work, as was our routine in the ICU. I was horrified when I saw the microbiology report of the culture samples taken from his leg. The report was dated more than twenty-four hours prior to my reading it. It listed the name of the bacteria identified from his leg wound and the names of the major antibiotics commonly used at that time, with a letter *R* or *S* after each. The letters stand for *resistant* and *sensitive*. The antibiotic he was on had an *R* after it. *Oh God*, I thought as I paged the resident on duty. *He is on the wrong antibiotic and I hope it is not too late, he is in a life-death situation because of the infection.* The resident was very rattled when he realized what happened, and he immediately ordered a new antibiotic. Apparently, the floor nurse had never had the time to look at the lab reports. Clerks on the floor who received and filed the reports were lay people; they were clueless. I couldn't figure out how this had been missed by the residents though. I should have looked to see what doctor wrote the last progress note on the chart, and when he wrote it.

The sixty-year-old man went into renal failure from the infection and died. His death had a huge impact on me, and it even crossed my mind to send the family an anonymous letter telling them to get a lawyer. I didn't do it, but I did talk about the case with the nursing supervisor. This hospital was known for its cardiovascular services, and this was a quality issue. She listened, but I never received any feedback. Not that I really expected it, since I was a staff nurse.

It was winter, and the city had one of its worst blizzards in decades. Everything was shut down; the roads were impassable. My car sat outside, and I had to unfreeze the lock on the door with a blow-dryer plugged into an extension cord that, in turn, was plugged into an outlet in my front hall. I was no more than a mile or two from home when I slid off the road, along with several other cars. I was able to get out of the shallow ditch, but was too frightened to continue, so I turned around to go home. After I arrived home I received a call from work. They were desperate: almost no one had been able to get to the ICU. Intensive care nursing takes special training, and they usually don't pull a nurse off the medical floor to fill in. They said they were sending the National Guard to pick up nurses. Two guys in a jeep arrived shortly afterward.

I worked a double shift before replacement nurses were finally able to make it in. The hospital offered us empty patient rooms if we wanted to stay over and sleep. I wanted to go home, but I didn't know how I would get there. The National Guard was not providing rides home. Fortunately, and unbelievably, the city bus was running. I was the only passenger, and the bus driver did something exceptional: he veered from his route and got me closer to home before dropping me off. The snow was deep, but I didn't have to walk far because of the bus driver's kindness.

An orthopedic doctor on staff at the hospital was admitted to the ICU after undergoing an operation to treat his cancer. A nonstop parade of physicians came into the unit for information and to wish him well. I think it was a shock to them that one of their own was in the same position as the other patients. The nurses pulled the curtains around his bed and shooed the non-attending doctors away. He was very ill and vulnerable. He did eventually die in the same hospital where he had served so long and well.

We had many successes, but there were patients we could not cure, and they fought for their dignity with every bit of strength they could muster. The doctors placed tubes in their bodies, and the patients tried to pull them out. To keep the tubes in, we were expected to restrain the patients using cloth restraints tied to the bed rails. I absolutely hated this. One day, a patient mouthed to me, please let me die. I told this to the resident on call when he was making his rounds. He said to me, "Why don't you accidently trip over the plug to the respirator." A coworker overhearing his statement said, "Why don't you get a Do Not Resuscitate order."

One day, I called in sick, a rarity for me. I just couldn't go in to clean and turn the almost dead. It was overwhelming.

CHAPTER FOURTEEN

Infection Control

———•◆•———

1979

I finally met my Joe Gannon. He had an MBA, not an MD, after his name, which was all right with me, it brought balance to my life. We did not discuss medicine night and day, and he wouldn't have impossible hours. At this same time an interesting career opportunity presented itself.

The hospital employed a nurse in a position called Infection Control Coordinator. She reviewed the records of all the hospital's patients with blood and wound infections to determine if the infections were hospital acquired. The infection information came from the microbiology lab. Hospital-acquired infections, called nosocomial infections, were recorded and factored into the monthly infection rate for specific areas of the hospital, such as the ICU, the newborn nurseries, the surgical units, and the dialysis unit. The infection rates were reported to a hospital committee. It was the committee's responsibility to review policies and procedures, and to intervene if infection rates were higher than national standards. The infection control coordinator also kept a record of patients with a "reportable" communicable disease and notified the health department. The coordinator's most important duty was to train the hospital staff to observe policies and procedures to prevent the spread of infection. I talked with the current coordinator many times when she visited our unit; one day, she informed me they were adding a position.

The responsibilities of the job were something new to me and very interesting. We started our days with a computer print-out from the microbiology department. We circled the positive blood and wound cultures and any other positive cultures with unusual bacteria not frequently seen in the hospital. We talked with the head nurses on the units to see if they had patients with communicable diseases or wound infections that needed special handling. We provided yearly training programs with an emphasis on hand washing.

My mentor was great, I could not have asked for a better teacher. I began to read literature about communicable diseases and hospital infections. I learned the indications for the different categories of antibiotics. I also learned that the Eli Lilly sales representative, who stopped by our office intermittently, lived across the street from one of our top surgeons. There was money in pharmaceutical peddling, even back then. We met sales people who sold medical equipment, and we made recommendations to the infection control committee when we saw something we really liked. I learned one of the most important areas in the hospital is some-times overlooked, the central processing unit. This unit is where equipment is cleaned and sterilized. Obviously, it was of the utmost importance that instruments provided for surgery were sterile. Test vials were regularly run in the sterilizers to ensure their performance was as it should be. A positive result from a test vial that had been run in a sterilizer was a huge red flag; the problem was addressed immediately. In the dialysis unit we tested the water baths, because dialysis patients are not able to fight off infection like the rest of the population. Most problems went away when we informed the staff there was a problem and reviewed policies and procedures with them.

Even today, public health departments rely on data from hospitals and doctors' offices to identify epidemics. When a recall for a food product is announced, it happens because the public health departments received multiple reports of gastrointestinal illness in patients at hospitals and doctors' offices. We had a list of what we were required to report. It covered diseases like tuberculosis (TB), sexually transmitted diseases (STDs), meningitis, and various gastrointestinal "bugs." Hospitals were very conscientious about reporting. I had my doubts about reporting from the doctors' offices, because they were increasingly being staffed with medical assistants instead of nurses. Medical assistants had, at best, a few months of training, sometimes even less. I would bet their training did not include public health or microbiology.

My mentor and I reported to the head of the laboratory, who was an MD, instead of to the director of nursing. He was a pathologist and probably in his late fifties. He had white hair, wore glasses, and had blotchy skin. He also had a red nose with prominent spider web like veins. To my eyes, he looked like a drinker. His most noticeable physical characteristic was his oversized stomach, which rested over his birdlike legs. His usual short-sleeved white shirt always looked wrinkled; a portion of it was frequently not tucked into his low pants. He was arrogant, and his communication style could only be described as demeaning.

We did not have to deal with him directly too often, usually only if there was a pattern of infections, or if we needed to discuss the agenda before the infection control committee meeting. He was the chairman of the committee but contributed little. My coworker wrote the agenda, spoke at the meeting, and prodded the other physicians on the committee to respond to problems. His input was usually nothing, or criticism. Most of the people in the lab went out of their way to stay out of his path.

The hospital had devised a system to track infections in the newborn's nursery. We sent postcards to pediatricians' offices and asked them to fill them out and mail them back if there were any significant finding at the baby's first checkup. We received a few cards reporting babies were coming into the offices with pustules. After we received a several more cards reporting the same thing, we brought the information to our boss. He was not impressed and dismissed us. When we finally had a total of twenty cards reporting pustules, we returned to him, and this time he had to agree something was going on. The laboratory tests showed the babies were infected with *Staphylococcus aureus*. We temporarily closed the nursery and scrubbed it down. We reviewed hand washing with all staff members on all shifts.

The cards stopped coming. We had done our job.

The ICU was always a potential hotbed for infection. Any tube inserted into the body increased the chances of a patient developing an infection. Also, many of our patients had serious underlying disease that predisposed them to infection.

We regularly saw patterns of infection in the unit. Patients who were recovering next to each other were growing the same bacteria in their lungs or their wounds. There were sinks in the front and back of the room, and in the private rooms, too, but not between the patient beds. When a patient coughed off the tubing connecting him to his respirator, it was a stretch to expect the nurse to run to the front of the room and wash her hands before reconnecting the patient. The nursing staff did the best they could, but the lack of sinks probably was a factor in the spread of infections. Hand-sanitizing products had not yet been developed. Today intensive care units have been redesigned to include a sink at every bedside.

When we noticed several sternal wound infections caused by the same bacteria in patients who had undergone open-heart surgery, we first alerted the ICU nurses then put on our scrubs and stood in the corner to observe an open-heart operation. We focused on how the nurses and the doctors handled the various pieces of surgical equipment. We did not notice anything problematic, but the infections stopped. My mentor said this frequently happens, because people try harder when they know they are being observed.

Several nurses on one of the medical units complained about an itchy rash on their hands. They had a patient with scabies on their unit, and they thought they had picked up his "germs." Scabies is a contagious and itchy skin condition caused by mites. We reported the complaints to our boss. Once again, his response was dismissive. I recorded additional complaints and returned to my boss and tried again. The nurses were then seen by a dermatologist, and the diagnosis of scabies was confirmed.

I enjoyed giving infection control classes. We provided a little hocus-pocus at the start of every class. We put powder on our hands that was visible only with a special lamp called a dark lamp. We always shook some of the hands of the class participants and then, later, turned off the lights and brought out the dark lamp to show everyone the "germs" they had acquired by shaking our hands. It always brought a gasp from the audience.

We had a regular lunch group composed of lab technicians, an administrative assistant, and a couple of pathologists. One day, the word at lunch was that an unnamed nun had entered the office of our boss, found booze, and had given him a tongue-lashing. I asked how that could be and was told, "The sisters own this hospital, never forget that." I thought *too bad they didn't fire him*, but I guess his contract kept that from happening. There was also gossip that he had been such a SOB at his last job that when he left, the staff rented a ballroom and threw a party.

One day, my elderly neighbor was admitted to the hospital by the squad after collapsing at home. I went to the ward to see him. I was shocked at his appearance. He had huge bruises on his arms, and his tongue looked black. He was on a blood thinner, and the laboratory test used to monitor the drug showed a dangerous level before his admission. The lab technician had documented that she reported his abnormal bleeding test to his physician expeditiously, saying it was a critical lab result. His physician, who was as old as my neighbor, did not call my neighbor and tell him to stop taking the drug. Maybe he just forgot. I was concerned and felt I had to report the episode to someone. I went to one of the other pathologists in the lab and told him what happened. I would not have dreamed of going to my ogre of a boss. I have no idea if anything was done in response to this error, but at least I had done my part to help improve patient care.

My mentor said she was tired of being psychologically browbeaten by our boss and that she was leaving her position. She said she was tired of doctors in general and did not wish to work for one ever again.

I was upset. My mentor was a smart professional. There wasn't a single administrative person in the hospital who did not know and respect her. Her departure was a big loss for the hospital. Of course, she's the one who ended up leaving, while the abusive doctor stayed.

A younger new nurse took my mentor's place. It wasn't long before she, too, developed anxiety from dealing with our boss. She left, and another nurse was hired. Then an infectious disease specialist with an MD was hired to manage the department.

While he seemed nice, I ultimately decided to return to patient care. I accepted a position in the Ambulatory Care department at the hospital.

Before my new ambulatory care job started, I took a week off to work as a camp nurse. Nursing magazines always included ads for camp nurses, and I thought it sounded like fun. I had heard about the job through a friend, and I took it out of curiosity and for the fun, not for the money: I was paid a token $100 for the week.

The camp was at a convent out in the country. It was a large nineteenth-century building set on several acres. When I arrived, two young women in Bermuda shorts and tennis shoes greeted me. They introduced themselves as nuns, and I was so amazed by their clothing that I commented on it. They were amused and assured me the habit was no longer mandatory in their personal lives.

The nuns showed me to my room, which was huge, with high ceilings and antique furniture, just like in nursing school. I was pleased to see nice, big windows allowed breezes to pass through, because the building had no air-conditioning. The nuns also showed me the first aid clinic, which was truly dated, looking like something from the previous century.

As we toured the building, I noticed that most of the nuns were much older and adhered to the traditional habit and veil. We went through the large common dining room and passed into the kitchen, where the nuns pointed out a large freezer chest, like the kind in a convenient market. It was loaded with ice cream, and they told me to help myself whenever I wanted. What a deal—all the ice cream I wanted!

As we finished our first evening meal I noticed all the diners carrying their plates to a counter with a dishpan full of soapy water. Then each person proceeded to wash only their plate and silverware and put them away. When I asked about this the young nuns laughed. They told me this system prevented conflicts from arising about whose turn it was to do the dishes. I thought to myself: *Nuns fight about dishes?*

The week was a blast. I was outside with the kids and the young nuns, playing ball and doing crafts the whole time. The kids had a few lumps, bumps, and scrapes but nothing serious. They were all about ten years old and did not cause any problems.

One night, as I was lying in bed, two bodies covered in white beds sheets stole into my room. They told me they were the ghosts of Saint So-And-So. Of course, it was only two of my new friends, and I had a good laugh.

At the end of the week, before leaving, I wandered the property and noticed a tiny cemetery for the nuns who had passed over the years. Many had lived to a ripe old age—despite their ice cream habits.

What a great week. I would have done the job for free.

CHAPTER FIFTEEN

Ambulatory Care

1984

I couldn't imagine why I had been given the job in ambulatory care in the blink of an eye. It was a day job, and people usually lined up for them. I soon learned that the surgeon who used the area the most was "difficult" and somewhat abrasive at times. This was common knowledge, except in the Infection Control department. Anyway, I did enjoy talking with patients again.

One of my duties was to administer a liquid preparation to patients   undergoing a colonoscopy. I also assisted with simple operations that were performed with a local anesthetic. I bandaged and gave post-op instructions. I also administered IV therapies and blood transfusions for outpatients with cancer, diabetes, and multiple sclerosis.

One of my regulars was a young girl with uncontrolled diabetes. Despite diligent physician monitoring and strict compliance with a "diabetic diet," her blood sugar levels were continually high. She was in her twenties, and, according to her physicians, already showed signs of kidney damage. Genetics were in play here; there was nothing this little gal did or did not do to have this condition. Unfortunately, her quality of life was very much ruled by the disease.

When she came into the department, I started her on an IV to hydrate her and provide insulin. Her mother was always with her; she sat on a chair in the department, knitting. We came to know each other quite well, and her mom shared some treasured Italian recipes.

A nice, dignified eighty-year-old woman came into our department for blood transfusions. She was slowly dying from metastatic cancer, and the transfusions were the only treatment she would agree to. She said she had watched her husband endure horrible side effects from chemotherapy, and she had decided, because of her age, to let nature take its course. She said she usually didn't feel ill, she just grew tired when she became too anemic.

A thirty-something woman with multiple sclerosis was also a regular. She came in for steroid infusions. She was nice, talkative, and was married to a professional football player. She told me it was very problematic finding clothing to fit him. Shirts would not close around his neck, sleeves were too tight, and ties were always ridiculously short.

I had patients of all ages and walks of life. An elderly man I was prepping for a colonoscopy turned out to be a veteran who told me that he had chronic bowel problems ever since being in the service. Incredibly he was one of the survivors of the Bataan Death March during World War II!

The ambulatory care department was next to the GI department and the ER. When the ER was too crowded, the ER's physician assistants used to borrow one of our tables to use for suturing their patients. They did most of the suturing.

One day an indigent patient came in with dog bites to his face and lip. The wounds went through the border of his lip; this met criteria for calling a plastic surgeon.

All the plastic surgeons we called that day were mysteriously busy and unable to take the patient. The medical caste system was well established: the surgeons did not want to deal with an uninsured patient. After several hours, the patient was turned over to a physician assistant who would perform the repairs. This patient was fortunate; the assistant on that day had a knack for sewing; he did an incredibly good job. (I saw the result when the patient returned to have his stitches removed.)

The nurses working in the GI department helped the doctors perform endoscopy procedures; they also cleaned the scopes afterward. A sigmoidoscopy is a procedure that checks the patient's rectum with a short scope. It is different from a colonoscopy because it does not require the use an anesthetic. A special table, called a Ritter table, tilts, so that the patient's bottom is tilted up and his head is tilted down. I was told a sigmoid exam was not particularly uncomfortable but certainly not something anyone looks forward to, given the compromising position. The GI nurses were good-natured, and they designed a badge for the patients to wear after undergoing the procedure: "I survived the Ritter table."

The "difficult" surgeon performed "lump and bump" removals at least several times a week. He also took care of clogged feeding tubes in nursing home patients. The rubber feeding tubes were threaded through an incision in the patient's abdominal wall and stomach then anchored with stitches. I paid attention to what the surgeon used to unclog the tubes and went out of my way to make certain I had the right guide wires and stitching material that he liked to use. He was usually short with me, and there was never any personal conversation between us. I had heard from my colleagues around the hospital that he was technically excellent, but it still didn't negate the uncomfortable feeling I had when I assisted him.

Sure enough, one day I came to work wearing maternity clothes. He looked at me and said, "Just great, this means you'll be leaving!" I was thrilled to be pregnant. Another nurse friend and I had been trying for almost a year. We even made jokes about visiting each other in the old folk's home if we never had children. I couldn't think of anything to say to the surgeon, so I didn't reply, but later I shared his comments with the GI nurses. One of them had known the surgeon for several years and said, "Oh, he's *really* upset you're pregnant and might leave, he just *loves* you!"

I said, "You've got to be kidding, the man has barely said a civil word to me since I've worked here!"

Surgeons! What can I say? They certainly aren't known for their people skills!

CHAPTER SIXTEEN

Recovery Room

———◆———

1986

I was just shy of ten years at the hospital when we had a son and I stayed home for a few months. My husband—the MBA I had met when I was working in infection control—then accepted a job offer out of town, so I did not return to my job. We were moving.

Once we had moved into our new home and the boxes were finally unpacked, I went to human resources (HR) at the local hospital to apply for a job. It was still simple in those days. I filled out two pages of forms, presented my nursing license, and the HR person called someone from nursing administration to speak with me. She reviewed what openings they had and asked when I wanted to start. No position in infection control was open, nor were there any openings in the ER. So I agreed to work in the recovery room. I didn't have to wait for weeks or months for a job offer. I didn't have to be fingerprinted or take a drug test. What the heck is happening in this country, when a licensed professional is assumed to be a criminal until proven otherwise?

There were no windows in the recovery room. It's a small thing, but working in a windowless environment has always bothered me. I had not been in a recovery room except for a brief period as a student nurse; there were new things for me to learn. One of them was that children wake up from anesthesia differently than adults. They awakened very irritable, and they often thrashed about the bed. It took two nurses to ensure they didn't fall off the bed or pull their IV out.

I also learned to use a small device to measure the respiratory output from the tube inserted into patients for anesthesia during their operation. The measurement from the device determined the patient's readiness to have the tube removed.

I was working evenings with just one other nurse; my patient at this time was an eighteen-year-old who had undergone an appendectomy. He was ready to have his tube removed, so that was what I did. He immediately went into what is called a laryngospasm—his vocal chords were seizing and closing off his oxygen supply. The guy turned blue. I hit the emergency button at his bedside and my coworker arrived…but no one else did. Fortunately, his spasm resolved spontaneously, and he was fine. I learned that hospitals are not always appropriately staffed on the off shifts. People in suits from administration dictate staffing levels according to something called a case mix index. What the administrators don't understand is that one patient can become critical and change the whole equation in an instant. Watching a patient have a laryngospasm was a very scary experience for me, which I shared with an anesthesiologist the next day. He instructed me on the appropriate response—using a large facial mask for the patient to breathe through, called an Ambu bag, (a piece of equipment that moves air into lungs better than mouth to mouth resuscitation)—if I ran into the situation again.

The recovery room nurses sometimes helped with the "same day" surgery patients. The patients started arriving at five-thirty A.M., and we showed them where to undress and had them sign all the pertinent forms before starting their IV solution in preparation for surgery. We also looked over all the lab results, circling abnormalities for the physicians in anesthesia to review. The nurses prepared a muscle relaxant and an opiate in syringes for anesthesia to administer to the patients. These drugs are controlled substances and must be signed for by the registered nurses. Any amount that is leftover is squirted into the sink while witnessed by another nurse, and the wasted amount is recorded. One anesthesiologist insisted that the leftover drugs be given to her for use in the operating room. None of the other anesthesiologists ever requested this. It wasn't that her request was so unusual but rather the way she made the request. She made such a big deal about it. Something about her manner bothered me, and for the first time in my career I thought she might be a user. I kept my suspicions to myself, because how could I prove anything?

One day, a memorable lady came in to undergo facial plastic surgery. She told me she was embarrassed that she was having her "eyes" done. I didn't really have an opinion—and offered none. Then she told me she had cried her face into its drooped condition. She said her daughter was murdered. Now I *really* didn't know what to say. Surgery might help the tissue around her eyes, but I knew the real problem was the pain in her soul—and she was in the wrong place for that kind of repair.

I was sitting next to a coworker who was on the phone at the nurse's desk in the recovery room. It was early morning. The first patient had not come out from the operating room, so we had no patients. My coworker was trying to get someone to clean up tree limbs in her yard that had fallen during a recent storm. "Get out of town, I save lives for fifteen!" she bristled to someone on the phone. When she hung up she informed me the tree folks wanted seventy-five dollars an hour. I shared her indignation.

She was a hoot. On another day she was reliving her personal experience as a patient in labor and delivery. She said the experience stripped her of both her modesty and her dignity: so many people were waltzing in and out of her room while someone was sticking a hand up her vagina to measure her progress. Summarizing her thoughts, she said to me, " Maintenance man, trash collector come on in, never mind my legs are parted and we are in the middle of *something* here. "

What she said rang true. There was a positive side to a nurse becoming a patient. It made you a more sensitive nurse.

CHAPTER SEVENTEEN

Emergency in the Suburbs

———————◆———————

1988

A position opened in the emergency room and I applied. Apparently, I missed my adrenaline fix. It had been a few years, but I had not forgotten the basics of the job.

It was late April. A beautiful evening for prom night at the local high school. The squawk box informed us the squad was bringing in four teenagers involved in an automobile accident. It was only eight P.M. Too early for drinking and driving.

In fact, the unfortunate car with the two couples had been on the way to the prom. No alcohol was involved though. Stuff happens. Fortunately, the kids were not seriously injured. They had bumps and bruises. Only one of the four needed stitches, and his shirt was bloodied. My coworker, an experienced mother of teens, walked in the room and took control of the situation. She had the boy remove his shirt. Then she took the shirt to the scrub sink and doused it with peroxide, and then water. *Presto!* The shirt was wet but clean. The boy put the shirt back on and headed out to the prom as originally planned, this time using parental transportation.

Just before eleven o'clock, another prom-goer arrived. He had been drinking…a lot. His blood alcohol level was almost double the legal limit, and he was barely alert, with impaired breathing. He vomited up copious amounts of fluid, but this did not perk him up. The physician had to insert a plastic breathing tube into his mouth, so he could be hooked up to a respirator. One of the nurses called the boy's parents and they arrived shortly after. When they saw their son on a respirator they were very upset, although we reassured them all indications pointed to a full recovery when the alcohol wore off. He was admitted to the ICU because he was on the respirator. I called housekeeping to come and mop the floor after we transported him to the ICU. This was customary, but the person on duty that night informed me their department did not clean up bodily fluids. I was too busy to argue, so I threw several towels on the floor, mopping the floor with my feet. This was clearly not one of the perks of the job. Most nights, I came home with blood, hair, tape and whatnot on my shoes. My shoes told the story of my work on any given day. I always left them by the door to the garage in our laundry room, to be cleaned up the next day.

It was the Fourth of July, and I entered work through the ambulance entrance. Most of the hospital nurses entered through the main entrance to the hospital but the parking lot was so much closer to the sliding door used to admit ambulance patients to the ER than the front door and the ER nurses always came in this way. Tom, one of my coworkers (and the only male RN), was outside the doorway, lighting a miniature charcoal grill. I had to laugh. No one on the day shift would dream of doing such a thing! The lack of interference from members of the hospital hierarchy was one of the perks of this holiday evening shift, they did not have to work holidays.

The ambulance doors faced west, looking out over an open field. Some evenings, time permitting, we could see the most magnificent sunsets. The weather that evening was beautiful, and it seemed we might have a pretty good night.

The emergency squad arrived. They had a middle school-aged boy on their stretcher. The boy has lacerations on his arm that were covered with bandages. There were also two other younger boys in tow uninjured, but too young to be left home alone. The boy with the cuts was supposed to be the babysitter for his brothers. The paramedic explained the kids were the sons one of his coworkers, another fireman, and they had broken a large aquarium leaving a "whole lot of water" on the floor at the home. The boy's cut was deep and involved muscle tissue, but the bleeding was controlled, so we could momentarily relax. His parents were on their way. Their first evening out without a hired babysitter had been abruptly halted!

To foster team spirit, all the new RNs were scheduled to spend a day riding with the firemen. They were trained emergency medical technicians in addition to being firemen and they were the people we communicated with via a radio during medical emergencies. It was nice to understand the pre-hospital scenario and get to know them better. When my day came, I was given an orientation at the fire station. I was absolutely amazed at the amount of clothing the squad members had to wear to be prepared for every alarm and car accident, no matter the temperature outside. This was for their own protection, of course. They did so much more than just put out fires, however. They extracted people from their cars after accidents, so they needed the protection from broken glass and sharp metal shards. They also responded to toxic spills on the freeway (and elsewhere). Firefighting is a dangerous job; I thought they were heroes.

We were having a slow morning, no fires or accidents. The chief at the fire station took me to the kitchen to review the day's menu. Just then, we received what was called an invalid call. A young man who had one of those devastating neuromuscular diseases that bound him to a wheelchair, was unable to get out of the bathtub. He was cared for by his elderly mother and she did not have the wherewithal to lift him. We arrived at the house, and two of the firemen cheerfully helped him out. I had no idea they provided such a service. Apparently, such calls were not that uncommon.

Our next call was for a kid who was stuck in a stairway banister. We cruised to the home in the fire truck. It was a very nice neighborhood—and a very big house. We were greeted at the front door by a grim-faced mother. She led us upstairs to a stairway landing where we saw a boy who looked about six years old, lying on the floor. His head was stuck between the stairway posts. The sight was hilarious....What kids won't do! My team was very professional, and the mother was so serious, that I had to bite my tongue to keep from laughing out loud. Common sense would tell you that what went in should come out. One of the firemen calmed the kid and manipulated his head out of the posts. No charge, thank you very much!There were no fires that day. My last run was for someone who was having difficulty breathing. She was elderly and had a history of heart failure. When you use a stethoscope to listen to the lungs of someone in heart failure, you can hear a soft crackling, which means there is fluid in the lungs. The crackling sounds somewhat like rustling a plastic dry cleaner's bag.

We heard crackling in the elderly woman's lungs, so an IV and oxygen were started to prepare to transport her to the hospital. While in her home, I noticed a big bag of potato chips on her table and some canned soups sitting on the counter. This indicated she was eating salt and more salt, a huge no-no for people with congestive heart failure. We needed to better educate folks on how to manage their diseases at home.

Sometimes people came to the hospital by car when they should have called the squad. A ten-year-old boy arrived by car, literally sitting in a pool of blood in the back seat. He had been shot with a BB gun, which ordinarily would not cause too much concern, but his wound was right in the groin. There was so much blood that we thought there might be significant damage to a blood vessel. It was the nurse's job to keep pressure on any bleeding wound to see if it would stop bleeding. If that failed, the doctor might examine the wound to look for the source of the bleeding; then he would stich it. In this case, the bleeding ultimately stopped without surgical intervention, but it was a long hold. We called in a vascular surgeon for a consult, just to be on the safe side.

Boating accidents and drownings are numerous in the summer when a big lake is nearby. The squad called one day and notified us they were on their way in with a boy who had nearly drowned. They entered the doors with a teenage boy on the stretcher. He was sitting up and had on an oxygen mask. He looked scared and depleted. The physician and one of my coworkers and I were escorting the stretcher into a treatment room when the ER doctor asked, "How are you, son?" The boy whispered, "I can't feel my arms and legs." We exchanged alarmed glances. The doctor shouted out, "Get a cervical collar!" It was already too late. Not only could the boy not feel his arms and legs, he could not move them either.

The history we received from the squad was that he had been floating underwater and someone bumped into him. The rest of the details were sketchy, but we pieced together that this teenager was probably doing a somersault in water that was too shallow. He evidently broke his neck and was unable to surface. I stopped the neurosurgeon as he was walking toward the door on his way to the parking lot. I knew he had been in to see the patient, who was now in the ICU. He shook his head and said the prognosis was not good, though the young man would live.

Another young healthy life forever altered.

We didn't often see teenage girls with stomach pain being brought in by the squad. When they burst through the doors with a moaning, writhing large fifteen-year-old girl we were perplexed, until she shouted, "It's coming right now!"

My coworker and I looked at each other. We knew what was coming next, and it wasn't the stomach flu or a gallbladder attack.

As soon as the girl had been transferred to a table in the ER, my coworker grabbed one side of the underwear and I grabbed the other. Then we yanked and looked. We saw the top of a baby's head. I hurriedly left the room and went to the desk where the ER doctor was standing and writing notes. I interrupted him with a tap on the shoulder and quietly told him that we were having a baby in Room One. His eyes widened, and he darted to the room. I grabbed an obstetrical pack off a supply cart and told the clerk to page someone from OB (obstetrics) as well as the surgical resident on duty. (We didn't have OB residents at our hospital.)

The baby arrived before its time and wasn't breathing. The surgical resident gently handled the infant and attempted resuscitation while the ER doctor attended to the mother. We rarely delivered babies in the ER, and we had to scramble to find a breathing tube small enough for this premature infant. It was no use; we couldn't bring the tiny being back to life.

The teenager denied knowing she was pregnant. It was a long night for her and her parents.

It was the start of another shift. My first patient was complaining of pain in his left flank, which could indicate a kidney infection or another type of renal problem.

Whenever a patient complained of pain in a flank, to expedite the evaluation process the nurses always obtained a urine sample and sent it off to the lab before the patient was seen by the doctor. I walked the patient to the bathroom and found vomit in the sink. I had to direct the patient to another bathroom. Calling house-keeping would have been futile. They had bare-bones staffing in the evening, and their priority was to wash down the beds left empty by discharged patients, in preparation for new admissions. Even if they had decided to clean up bodily fluids that day, they might not have shown up for an hour. (Put another duty in the nurse's column: bathroom cleaning....What are these folks in administration and budgeting thinking?)

My next patient was a toddler. Her older brother said she had eaten a mushroom off the front lawn. I checked her vital signs, which were fine, and then gave her some ipecac disguised with juice to make her vomit. I gave the parents a large basin and instructed them to get her to drink as much water as possible to help the ipecac do its thing. Then I went to a small room where ER personnel could view something like an encyclopedia on microfilm, to see if I could find any information about wild mushrooms. It was 1990.

The clerk had a computer to use when we needed to order laboratory tests, but we didn't have a computer to conduct internet searches for poison. One of my coworkers called Poison Control, and they suggested we call the biology department at a local university. We made some calls but got no information. I wasn't ever able to find anything on lawn mushrooms on the microfilm, but the ipecac worked. The little girl went home with instructions for the parents to return if there was any change in her condition.

Children do some of the most unexpected and outrageous things. They get into medications, make-up, nail polish. I had one who bit into a toilet bowl deodorizer tablet. They also put small objects in their noses and ears, things like Barbie doll shoes and rocks. One night, a child presented with a complaint of "foreign body up the nose." An ER doctor with a sense of humor examined her then recorded on her chart: "Chief Complaint—Rock up Nose. Exam—Rock up Nose. Treatment—Remove Rock from Nose. Instructions—Keep Rocks out of Nose."

Parents also do some stupid things. A boy in middle school was injured during a school football game and was brought in by the squad. His X-ray showed a fractured femur—a very serious injury that would require surgery. It had been pouring rain most of the day, and the football field had to be a sea of mud. Why the game was not called off was beyond me. This was a middle school sporting event, not pro ball. I thought the risk of injury far outweighed any reason to play the game. I would have kept my kid home and talked with the coach. But that's just me.

It was a quiet night, which occasionally happened when something like the Super Bowl or a blockbuster movie was on TV. The nurses were sitting in the lounge, drinking coffee, looking at magazines, and sharing some stories about some crazy recent cases. We never shared names, of course, but how do you not comment on a complaint of a gerbil in a plastic bag up a rectum? When you think you've heard it all, you are wrong.

One of the OB doctors stopped in the lounge on his way out the door. He said that the OB doctors were now required to be certified in advanced cardiac life support. He said he didn't know what to do, because it had been such a long time since he was a resident and had done a medical rotation. One of my coworkers said, "I guess you'll do what the rest of us do, open the book and study."

None of us in ER really had to study; we administered cardiac life support very frequently. The hospital was situated among numerous nursing homes in the suburbs, and "ticker" problems (meaning heart problems) were among our most frequent complaints.

We were stumped. We had a twenty-eight-year-old female patient in a room with a monitor displaying an abnormal electrocardiogram. In fact, the electrocardiogram showed a waveform that appeared to be an acute injury pattern, which meant the patient seemed to be having a heart attack. She had come in complaining of chest pain, but heart attacks just don't happen to young women, unless, of course, drugs like cocaine were involved. However, she denied drug use.

One of the treatments for an acute heart attack, or myocardial infarction, is the administration of a clot buster. The ER doctor decided to talk with a cardiologist before going any further. The cardiologist came in and solved the mystery. The young lady had been on medication for migraines for over a year and had abruptly stopped taking the drug. The cardiologist believed that stopping the administration of the drug had caused the blood vessels in the patient's heart to "spasm"—but she did not have a heart attack. He saved her from receiving the clot busters and, in fact, her electrocardiogram reverted to normal the next day.

It was the weekend. I was in my kitchen baking cookies when suddenly I felt my heart thumping out of my chest at a very fast clip. What the heck was going on? I sat down on a kitchen chair and took my pulse. My heart rate was not only fast but irregular. I started to feel funny, almost panicky, and then the thumping stopped as quickly as it started. I decided to just wait and see if this peculiar episode repeated itself before I called my doctor. I was a young woman in my thirties and didn't have any health problems that I was aware of. Maybe I just had too much sugar from eating the cookie dough? The fast, irregular heartbeat occurred again while I was at work. I asked one of my coworkers to put me on the monitor and run a strip. The strip showed PVCs (premature ventricular contractions), which meant an area in my heart was firing off unexpectedly and was out of sync. People can have occasional PVCs without having anything seriously wrong with their hearts. I was having frequent PVCs. My blood pressure was normal, so I got dressed and took the strip to the ER doctor for his opinion. He was concerned. He told me if someone walked in off the street with this strip he would admit them. I told him I didn't want to be admitted but agreed to have my blood pressure checked throughout the evening and a follow-up appointment with a cardiologist.

On cue, while I was at the cardiologist's office, my heart went off again.

The cardiologist reviewed an electrocardiogram and declared me essentially healthy. He decided to take a "wait and see" attitude before starting medication to control my heart rhythm. I wasn't given a cardiac stress test, because it wasn't the standard of care at the time. And I never went on medication, because the episodes did not reoccur again. Several decades have passed, and I'm still here. So, I guess the moral of the story is: we can't always explain everything.

Some conditions do seem to have a clear explanation. An LOL ("little old lady") in NAD (no acute distress) was brought in by squad complaining of an upset stomach. A coworker and I were in the ER room, checking her out. Her vital signs were normal, she wasn't sweating, and the pattern on cardiac monitor looked normal. We told her she had to get undressed and put on a gown so that she could be seen by the doctor. She asked for some help, and then under her slacks and sweater we found a huge, tight girdle, the kind worn in the 1940s or 1950s. It was a struggle to peel off the girdle, and my coworker said, "This is like taking the casing off a sausage."

Once the girdle was off, the lady breathed a sigh of relief. Her pain vanished. We all had a good laugh; we believed we had found the cause of her stomach discomfort.

The squad came in with another LOL. She was about ninety years old and from a nursing home. She arrived in a curled-up position, and she was breathing through an oxygen mask. She had dementia and had been bedridden for years, so we were unable to obtain any information from her. The squad reported a heart rate of 40 beats per minute (a normal heart rate is 60 to 100 beats per minute). We hooked her up to a monitor as soon as she arrived and confirmed her heart rate was approximately 35 beats per minute; the electrical conduction system in her heart was not working properly. Her blood pressure was low, and her oxygen level was also low, even with the oxygen mask on.

We ordered all the routine laboratory tests and a cardiology consult. The cardiologist was in the house and came down to the ER promptly. He decided a pacemaker was needed and called the radiology department to schedule a time to insert one. Then a breathless woman arrived in the patient's room. She identified herself as the patient's daughter and emphatically said to the cardiologist, "Leave her alone! I don't want her picked on or resuscitated." The cardiologist started to argue with her, but she would not change her stance. He eventually left, and I wondered how and why the lady was even transferred to us.

Don't get me wrong. I'm convinced that patient diagnosis and prognosis is more important than the patient's biological age when offering treatment. This patient did not have significant cognitive function and, apparently, had been in this condition for years. The consensus among the nurses was to keep her comfortable and let nature take its course, as her daughter requested. We believed a pacemaker would only prolong the inevitable. Obviously, there were no advance directives in place. It is *so* important to get this taken care of before the emergency happens. We just need to do better.

It was the Sunday morning of Thanksgiving weekend. We had received a DOA, dead on arrival. The coroner was called because we could not reach the family doctor to confirm the patient's history. People with a terminal condition who die at home are usually released by the coroner and the family can then transfer the body to a funeral home, if the family doctor will sign the death certificate. A hearse and a smiling middle-aged man in a long black coat and wearing a hat arrived very quickly. He was so cheerful picking up the body that a coworker and I commented to him about this. We said it was nice to see a smiling face under such difficult circumstances. He said he was always happy working on holiday weekends because he made $60 an hour "picking up stiffs." His words, not mine. We were appalled; we saved lives for $16 an hour.

Fortunately, in the ER, just when you are appalled and fed up another patient arrives and provides comic relief.

I was helping with a pelvic exam. A young lady came in with lower abdominal pain and had to have a swab taken to check for infection. She said she was mortified and put the sheet over her head while the doctor did the gynecologic exam. I assured her we did this all the time and he would not recognize her if he saw her on the street the next day. She finally calmed down and pulled the sheet away from her face before the doctor left. We all looked at each other and laughed.

A patient came in with a nosebleed; this one got a pat on the back from the nurses. He was holding a large metal mixing bowl to collect the blood coming through the washcloth he was holding to his nose with his other hand. We appreciated the containment and sat him on a stretcher so we could apply firm, constant pressure to the bridge of his nose to try to stop the bleeding. Most people do not apply the pressure correctly (or long enough) to see if the bleeding will stop; instead, they just head to the ER. The best we could do with this patient was to slow the flow; he had to have his nose packed with gauze. Sometimes we cannot get the bleeding stopped even with packing, in which case we call in an ENT (ear, nose and throat) doctor. Calling in a specialist was not customary; the ER doctors did a good job resolving most nosebleeds.

There was sometimes a dilemma handling patients with lacerations on their face. The hospital was in an affluent area, so it was not unusual for the patients—or the parents of patients—to inquire about the need for a plastic surgeon for a facial injury. If the cut was straight, not ragged, and did not pass through the border of the patient's lip, an experienced ER doctor would usually sew the wound with a fine-gauge suture that would leave minimal scarring. But if any patient (or parent of a minor) asked the doctor if they thought there was a need for a plastic surgeon, some automatically said, "Yes." In a typical case, the doctor's thought process was: *This patient probably has unrealistic expectations about the outcome of suturing and will always wonder if they were misled by not having a plastic surgeon called in.*

Suturing small children was a challenge for the nursing staff. Even when we knew a small child's wound had been numbed with the local anesthetic, the patient still screamed and fought. Sometimes my forearms went numb from holding the child's face still, so they could be stitched. They obviously wanted to be held by a parent, but when the parent was crying, it increased the child's stress even more. Sometimes it would have been best if the parent had just stayed in the waiting room.

When I started my shift with a request by the head nurse to come to her office I immediately felt anxious. Most nurses who were called into the office were in trouble for something. I wasn't in trouble; instead, the head nurse had been instructed to compliment me on my excellent documentation regarding a patient with chest pain. Apparently, the patient had complained about something after discharge, so the record was pulled and looked over by the powers that be. Our head ER physician had the habit of cutting corners and writing under the "History" section the words "As Above"—meaning, read the nurse's notes. He followed this with a one-sentence physical assessment. My note had provided a clear picture of the patient's condition that had let the ER physician "off the hook". Good for me, but shame on him for his *poor* documentation. His habits were noticed by the other nurses, too. One of my coworkers went to administration and complained that the doctor sometimes stood at the door and never even laid a stethoscope on chest pain patients, just ordered tests. My coworker resigned shortly thereafter. I did not know her well, so I never got any story from her about her abrupt resignation.

A policeman came in one evening and asked to speak to one of my coworkers. When she walked over to him, he immediately offered his hand and sincere thanks for her excellent documentation. It had been the tipping factor in a court hearing for an assault complaint. A woman had answered an ad for a secretarial job at a private home. The man answering the door proceeded to hit her a few times before she had been able to escape. In court, the man denied hitting her, and the doctor's notes had not been helpful. The nurse, however, had documented a reddened, swollen cheek. The man was found guilty.

Once again, I observed that some of the ER doctors are fast and some take their time or, rather, give more time to individual patients. If the patient load was too high and the patients had to wait more than an hour just to be seen, the ER doctor on duty was supposed to call in his designated backup. Most of the ER doctors, however, were reluctant to call in the backup. I'm not sure if it was an ego thing or a compensation thing, but when there was a long wait in the ER it made things awkward for the nursing staff.

The squad came in with a young man in his early twenties. He had a history of depression and had taken an overdose of his prescription medication for depression. This was a serious problem, because the medication was a type of drug called a tricyclic, and an overdose could cause a chaotic heart rhythm that was incompatible with life. Even worse, there was no antidote for the drug. I often wondered why it was prescribed, given the risk, because previously in my career I had seen a patient who overdosed on the same drug, and he had died.

The young man who had been brought in by the squad was talking, but his heart soon started showing signs of irritation. He went into cardiac arrest. We placed him on a respirator then gave him multiple medications to calm his heart.

While we worked on the patient who had overdosed the department became hopelessly backed up. The ER doc was not ready to "Call It"; I fully understood. We had talked to this patient. The doctor asked me to call in his backup, which I did. The backup physician wanted to know why we were backed up, so I told him. There was a pause at the other end of the phone, and then the backup physician said, "Well, he's a dead man, tell him—" meaning the ER doctor currently on duty "—to stop and move on to the other patients." I was appalled and suggested he relay his message to the ER doctor himself.

We all grow hardened, it seems. The patient did die, and it was heartbreaking.

A new CEO took over the hospital shortly after that incident. He was very conscious of public relations and gave the charge nurse on every shift the authority to call in a backup physician; no permission was needed from the physician on duty. We were all grateful.

One day when I was off duty and driving a commercial suddenly came on my car radio about my hospital's emergency room. It said the new room for patients with chest pain was now open, with trained staff who could promptly handle any cardiac emergency. When I reported for my next shift, all the nurses were talking about the commercial in the lounge. We were laughing since NOTHING had changed in our department. We used the same room for patients with complaints of chest pain we had always used. The staff was the same. Our treatment was the same. We wondered what administrative personnel had thought this one up. Too bad they weren't spending some of the money on extra house-keeping personnel.

The squad came in with another DOA. We quietly directed them to put the body in a small room called the cast room, where we made splints and casts. I taped a piece of paper over the window in the door so no one wandering through the department could inadvertently see in.

The victim was a presumed suicide. He was young, maybe forty. There were marks around his neck; he had been found hanged. The squad started an IV but knew he was dead and had not pursued any other measures. He supposedly did not have any family and was found by a neighbor. Wadded-up paper was sticking out of his pants pocket. I removed it and was horrified to see that it was discharge instructions from another emergency room, written up several hours earlier. He had apparently gone to that ER complaining of depression and was discharged with a referral to an outpatient counseling center and a prescription. Who knows what he told them…or if they really dropped the ball.

What a tragedy! So many people are struggling to stay alive just another day with catastrophic diseases, and then we see a suicide.

We called the coroner, and he asked us to bag the hands. We followed the instructions and left everything as it was when he arrived for the pickup. Before I finished my shift, I called the other ER and spoke with the doctor who had seen the deceased. I reported what happened, just in case something could have been done differently. The ER doctor seemed shaken and thanked me for my call.

Today, I think there are a lot more people with serious mental health problems walking the streets than there were just ten years earlier. I've not seen data to support this, it's just my observation. We have reduced the number of mental health hospitals, and perhaps there is a correlation between fewer of these hospitals being available for mental health patients and an increased rate of suicide.

I didn't cry that night. I guess I was becoming hardened. But I did think that maybe there was another job in nursing that would not be so mentally draining.

Generally, the nurses and doctors got along. We sometimes ate together in the cafeteria and shared stories about our families. Then a new physician joined the group of ER doctors. It didn't take long for the nurses to agree that he was going to be a problem.

The new physician was one of the slower doctors, He did not seem comfortable with surgical patients, and he did not like suggestions from the nursing staff. Nurses learn from doctors and most of our suggestions to him were based on the customary and usual practices by other doctors that we have worked with. A small child came in one night with a forearm that was obviously broken; there was angulation, the forearm was bent at an abnormal angle. The nurses splinted the arm and placed an ice bag on it. Because of the extent of the deformity, I knew we would be calling in an orthopedist that same night to straighten the arm. The child was crying with fright and pain. One by one the nurses went up to the new guy and said, "Did you want to order some pain medication?"

First, the new physician was annoyed. Then he became angrily adamant. He wasn't going to order *anything*. Instead, he was just going to wait for the orthopedist. This was obviously a doctor who needed to be in control of "his" emergency room.

The child waited almost two hours for the orthopedist to arrive and order pain medication. We all thought it was unacceptable.

I talked to the assistant director of the ER physicians a few days later. I told him a child with a broken arm came into the ER a few days ago, and the new doctor had not been comfortable medicating him. Additionally, I said, "If my child came in with an obviously deformed arm, I would expect him to receive some pain medication immediately."

The assistant director was a father and a very nice man. He talked to the problem doctor, and although the doctor became more amenable to giving pain medication, he was still dismissive to the nursing staff. It wouldn't be long before there was another incident.

A young woman came in complaining of abdominal and shoulder pain. Routine labs were ordered, including a pregnancy test, which is customary for young females with abdominal pain. The pregnancy test came back positive, and her blood count was within normal limits.

The woman was sent for a CAT scan, and within a half hour the CAT scan technician called me. She said that she had made several attempts to reach the radiologist on call, but he had not answered. She told me I should tell the ER doctor to come over and look at the film, because she thought the patient might have a belly full of blood. She said she was not allowed to comment about findings because she was a tech, but she was frightened for the patient.

It was possible the patient had a pregnancy in her fallopian tube. If her tube ruptured it would turn into a surgical emergency, because the patient would be in danger of hemorrhaging. I had seen cases like this several times. I immediately told the ER physician that the tech couldn't reach the radiologist and that she would like him to look at the CAT scan. I also expressed my concern about the woman's low blood pressure, even though we did have an IV going.

The ER doctor blew me off. He said he was waiting for the radiologist. Period.

Fifteen minutes passed—an eternity, as far as I was concerned. I tried to talk with the ER doctor again and threw out the comment, "What if she is bleeding from a tubal pregnancy, would you consider calling OB/GYN for an opinion?"

My question infuriated the doctor. Just as he was telling me off, the radiologist got on the phone, sounding the siren to get a surgeon in *now*. He confirmed the patient was bleeding in her abdomen.

The patient made it to surgery, but I was upset because this ER physician seemed to be another nonteam player. It is so difficult to helplessly watch when you feel everything is not being done for a patient in a timely manner. My coworkers also reported that it was difficult to communicate with this physician. The head nurse listened to our concerns and reported them to his superiors. Ultimately, he was let go.

The squawk box let us know the squad was on the way with a young woman in her thirties who had been found unconscious on her kitchen floor. They reported her vital signs and her posture on the floor in detail. Her arms were extended straight out, and her hands were clenched. Their description matched the posture a person with a severe brain injury assumes—a lesson I learned years ago. It sounded like she had a bleed—a hemorrhage. They didn't know if she fell and had hit her head or had a bleed first and then fell.

When the young woman arrived, she did not look good. She had to have a tube inserted in her throat to facilitate breathing. Her husband was called at work. He was a policeman, and when he arrived and saw her, he became faint. A man who saw the worst in life regularly on his job had not actually seen the worst until today.

I was called into the head nurse's office again. This time I was told a former patient of mine was complaining that I had ruptured the his ear drum while irrigating earwax out of his ear. There was a problem with the documentation, though, as the doctor hadn't documented anything after the irrigation; he had simply discharged the patient. I assumed the doctor had examined the patient but just forgot to write what he had found. But that doesn't cut it legally.

I was sent to an office in the administration department to give a statement about what I remembered. I felt very uncomfortable.

A few days later, the doctor on duty the day of the incident told me the patient had a hearing test, and the results were normal. Because a patient had to be injured to sue, the case was closed. What a relief! It was particularly comforting because I remembered a coworker's story about months of misery after being named in a lawsuit along with the hospital and doctor. In my coworker's case, an elderly patient had come to the ER moaning; he was in serious respiratory distress. The patient, a woman, had dementia, so she was not able to communicate. She was twisted up in a fetal position, like many admissions from long-term care facilities. The staff treated the respiratory problem…but it turned out the patient had a fractured hip, even though there was no history of injury. The nurse was not found to be at fault, but nothing negates the stress and self-doubt a prolonged lawsuit elicits.

After working six years in the community ER, I was ready to look for another job. Maybe the final straw was the suicide man, the one with the wadded-up discharge instructions in his pocket, or the wife of the policeman, or cleaning vomit out of bathroom sinks. I don't know. But one day I came home and asked my husband if I could stay home and be a housewife and mom for a few months and think about what to do next. He said it was fine.

CHAPTER EIGHTEEN

Quality Improvement

—————◆—————

I took my son to the local amusement park with the neighbors a week later; the children had just started their summer vacation. When we returned in the late afternoon, my husband was home. He had lost his job. I would be going back to work immediately.

An ad in the newspaper pitched an auditing position at a hospital a few miles away. While working at my previous ER job, I had assisted the nursing office in collecting some data for a city-wide study on bed usage in ICUs. I applied for the position and was hired, with a modest pay raise. It's kind of a shame I had to change jobs and hospitals to get that raise.

My new office was in the basement of the hospital and had no windows, but it had recently been updated with new carpet and new paint. I shared the room with five other nurses. My new coworkers were friendly, and the only negative I could see was walking past the "hide-a-body cart" every morning. When it wasn't in use, the cart was always parked in the hall outside our office. It brought back unpleasant memories.

I had several duties. One of them was to be the hospital's liaison for insurance companies that insured the ICU patients. I had to call them with clinical data to justify each patient's need to be in an ICU. I also collected data on all the open-heart surgery patients. The hospital was told by one of the major insurance companies that they needed to provide complication rates; otherwise there would be contractual ramifications. Even though it was 1992 and the hospital performed over two hundred open-heart procedures a year, they had never collected or analyzed outcomes associated with these cases. I recorded deaths, returns to surgery for bleeding, post-op infections, cardiac arrests, and strokes in all the heart-surgery patients. Nationwide data were available to see how we compared.

Word traveled fast. Some of the doctors were upset and were a bit snippy with me, if they showed up for rounds and I was looking at their chart. Fortunately, the data showed that our hospital performed well.

Some of nurses at the insurance company were also snippy with me. One day, when I called in about a comatose woman on a respirator, the insurance company's nurse said she would approve only one day in the ICU. I was truly annoyed. "Look," I said, "you and I both know this woman isn't going anywhere fast, except possibly to heaven. Why are you wasting your time and mine with another call tomorrow, at least give me a couple of days!"

I liked my new boss. We had something in common: we were both a bit outspoken. Shortly after I started, the infection control nurse at the hospital left, and I was offered her job, because I had previous experience in that position.

I started my day in the lab again obtaining a computer print-out of reports on patients' cultures, as I had in my previous infection control job. I then made rounds throughout the hospital to let the charge nurses know whether any patients in their units were harboring a particularly troublesome germ. Even with the development of so many new antibiotics, modern medicine was challenged to keep the upper hand over the microbial world. The bacteria were ever evolving.

Many (or at least most) hospitals printed out an annual compendium listing the species of bacteria that had been found in specimens cultured over the previous twelve months. The report included the resistance and sensitivity patterns of the bacteria to the most frequently used antibiotics. We called this an anti-biogram. I had saved an antibiogram from my infection control job ten years earlier, and there was a huge difference: the germs or bacteria (whichever term you wanted to call them) had become more resistant. This was a hot topic in medicine, and there was serious discussion about overuse of antibiotics, as overusing these medications was believed to be causing the resistance. Hospitals were now hiring infectious disease specialists to monitor resistance patterns and educate the physician staff on antibiotic use.

One category of antibiotics is called cephalosporins. Within this category there are many different formulations, each with a different name. Each formulation, or rendition, is designed to target specific bacteria. I was attending a class one day and the speaker, an infectious disease doctor, put up a slide that said, "Cepha who, Cepha what, and Cepha why." He was addressing the confusion about which cephalosporin to use. He said our favorite cephalosporin was Cepha lunch. That is, we used whichever product was being promoted by the drug representative who brought lunch. He was joking, of course, but there was that kernel of truth to what he said. The drug detail men, as they were called, not only visited doctor's offices but marched about the hospital at will, bringing food and goodies.

As in my previous infection control position, I ensured all reportable diseases were reported to the health department. The lab usually made the call, but I checked the call logbook. I also liked to know what was going around in the community. I recorded all surgical wound infections and positive blood cultures. Positive blood cultures meant the patient's infection was serious and widespread throughout the body, because it was present in the bloodstream. I recorded pertinent information about the patient and reported monthly to the infection control committee.

The hospital had an infectious outbreak while our infectious disease physician was on vacation and out of the country. I noticed several post-op patients had the same bacteria, *Staphylococcus aureus,* growing in their surgical wounds. When I reviewed their charts, I realized they all had vascular surgery and had been in the ICU before transferring to regular surgical floors. Then several patients in the ICU developed staph infections. The infections were in their wounds and in their blood. This was very serious, and I made an appointment to talk to one of the internal medicine physicians on staff about the situation. He was covering in the absence of our infectious disease doctor.

I sat in a chair in the conference room where we had agreed to meet. An administrative assistant was in the room cleaning up after its last use. There was a restroom off to the side of the room. We heard a toilet flush…but there was no water running afterward. Then the door to the bathroom opened and the doctor I was meeting with walked out. The administrative assistant and I looked at each other, and she quietly said, "His mother didn't teach him."

Unbelievable! I thought.   What was I supposed to say in response to this?

When I met with the doctor, I told him we had over a dozen cases of hospital-acquired post-op wound infections caused by *staph aureus* and that the commonality was the ICU. He was concerned, and we walked down to the ICU together to talk with the head nurse. I thought the physicians should be notified by a note being put in each of their mailboxes, but he didn't want to do that. Instead, he asked the head nurse to monitor who went into the rooms of the infected patients, and to watch who washed their hands afterward. Signs were also placed at all the bedsides, indicating contact isolation protocol was to be followed. This meant special attention had to be paid to hand washing, because the patients the physicians were examining had an infection. After one day, the head nurse reported that the biggest offenders—the people who were not washing their hands—were physicians and X-ray technicians.

I informed the X-ray supervisor. The doctor was responsible for notifying the physicians about the outbreak. I was not informed how this was accomplished, but I am sure the head nurse did remind all staff members including physicians about hand washing. When our infectious disease physician returned, he and I reviewed all the cases and the time frames for when the infections started. He hypothesized the index case—the first documented patient—was probably a respirator patient who had *staph* pneumonia. The germ can become airborne, and hospital personnel can be carriers without showing evidence of disease.

The infected patients were separated from the other patients. The pneumonia patient on the respirator was transferred to the floor. The outbreak stopped.

Hospitals voluntarily asked for accreditation from an independent organization called the Joint Commission on Accreditation of Healthcare Organizations, also known as JCAHO. They paid thousands of dollars for an outside team of physicians, nurses, and health administrators to review daily practices, policies, and procedures throughout the hospital. Accreditation was desirable; it was considered a validation of the quality of the services the hospital provided, and it was good PR. The surveyors focused on policies that addressed equipment processing, fire safety, patient safety, nursing, and physician documentation. Hospitals were given an approximate survey date and made a real effort to put their best foot forward for the survey. Hospitals had their staff education departments provide their personnel with additional training before the survey. I always thought a better picture of the quality at a facility would be obtained with a surprise visit.

Our hospital had a storage problem. Equipment was permanently parked in the halls: IV poles, wheelchairs, boxes of patient supplies like bandages, and so forth. There was real concern the hospital would lose accreditation points in this area, until some genius in administration solved the dilemma. A mover was hired to temporarily remove the equipment the day before the survey. It remained on the truck, driving around the city for the day and a half of the survey, and returned when the surveyors left. We passed our survey.

CHAPTER NINETEEN

Office Nurse

———◆———

My husband changed jobs, and we moved to another city out of state. I wanted an infection control job again, or at least an office job. It had been a nice break, not having to deal with life-and-death situations. I also loved having weekends off.

It was 1993, and the newspaper was still the primary place to search for employment—either that, or possibly a headhunter. The internet was just getting started. I combed the newspaper daily but found nothing. I put together my resume then drove around to office complexes in the area where I lived and dropped them off. Finally, I received a call from an urgent care center in walking distance from my home. They offered me a position with a 30 percent pay cut from what I had previously been making. Sometimes, you must draw the line—and I did in this instance: I kept looking.

When my CPR certification expired, I talked to a nursing staffing agency. They gave me information about where to take a CPR class. I had to renew my CPR certification if I wanted to work for an agency or in a hospital again.

I reported for an evening CPR class. The room was filled with middle-aged men. They were dentists obtaining mandatory certification. I got the impression they weren't thrilled to be there. In fact, I overheard one of them say that there wasn't a chance in hell he would ever perform mouth-to-mouth on anyone. I didn't mention that no one ever had to do this; instead, a manufactured airway surrounded with a plastic cuff could be placed in the patient's mouth. This device allowed air to be passed from the caregiver to the patient without the caregiver's mouth actually coming into contact with the patient's mouth. It was used by the squads and in the hospital, and was readily available commercially.

The instructor, a nurse, arrived with two practice dummies and a big black bag of equipment to help the dummies "breathe." The dentists were not particularly adept at performing CPR. The resuscitation dummy was designed to spit out a paper strip from the side of the chest; the paper strip showed electrical conduction in the pattern of a normal heart tracing if the CPR was being performed correctly. Tonight, it just was not happening. The instructor was alone with the dentists and me. Her assistant was a no-show. The teacher was becoming a bit overwhelmed by the task. I told her I was an ER nurse and sort of stepped in as an assistant. The dentists all ultimately passed and left. The instructor asked me, "Who are you? Do you want a job?" Then she handed me a card and told me to call the number.

She worked for a large medical group, and when I called I was asked to come in for an interview. The group provided the medical care for an HMO plan offered by a large insurance company in the city. The group had nine offices throughout the city, and I was hired to screen calls at one of the offices. I would provide advice according to a protocol or offer an appointment.

I had not yet completed my orientation when I received a phone call from the director of nursing, asking me to meet for lunch. She had somehow seen my resume and she noticed that I had previously done some quality improvement work and auditing. I had lunch with her and it was a done deal: I was now a quality improvement nurse. I would share an office with another nurse, namely, the QI (quality improvement) coordinator at the business headquarters. The office was in a high-rise in a very nice part of town; a beautiful high-rise with outstanding views.

The first thing I learned was that the quality complaints were recorded by hand; nothing was on computer. The medical group had over 90,000 members and 70 providers (doctors, nurse practitioners, and physician assistants). The job was unmanageable without computer tracking.

I knew how to perform basic word processing tasks so I asked one of the administrative assistants to teach me how to make a simple spreadsheet with Excel to track quality issues by date, complaint, provider, office, and resolution. My coworker and I were thrilled when we got the spreadsheet up and running. We received most of our information about potential quality issues from a group of nurses called utilization managers who tracked all our members who were hospitalized. They recorded things we termed "triggers" or "sentinel events," such as unexpected death, re-admission to the hospital within thirty days of discharge, and postoperative bleeding or infection. They also recorded any patient complaints about their care. We were moving forward in medicine; patients could question their care without their complaints automatically being dismissed.

Nothing is perfect; medicine is not an exact science. Medical treatments evolve and change over the years by trial and error, or from the development of better testing. Doctors and nurses do make mistakes. Patients are noncompliant with the treatments and medications doctors advise them to adhere to. Patients do not always provide complete information about themselves and their medications, which could affect the course of their treatment. Nevertheless, we all do the best we can.

My coworker and I recorded the triggers, sentinel events, and any complaints from providers or members. Then we trended them. That is, we conducted research to determine if our surgical outcomes were within published national standards. If we identified a pattern of poor outcomes, we referred the case to the medical director, and he decided whether the issue should be discussed with the risk management committee. That committee was composed of several doctors, a nurse practitioner, the quality nurses, the director of nursing, the CEO of the organization, and the attorney for the medical group.

At that time HMOs were starting to take some flack in the printed media and even became fodder for late night TV comedians. But I felt that, overall, we were providing really good care. Many of the issues that came up were the result of system failure and not the fault of one individual. There was a case when a patient's lab test results showed a potentially live threatening abnormal result; however, the patient could not be reached because we did not have a valid phone number. The patient eventually showed up at an ER in critical condition. We agonized over this event and then educated all company employees on how to handle the situation in the future. They were told to call the sheriff and to always check that the listed phone number was valid at every patient contact.

Another patient did not get notified that the results of her Pap smear were abnormal: the chart had been inadvertently filed without the obligatory physician initials indicating he or she had reviewed the lab report. We caught the error only when the patient returned with additional symptoms and then was diagnosed with cancer. We reviewed and revised our method of handling and documenting abnormal lab results. We provided employee education to help prevent a recurrence of the error. We also told patients to always follow up with their doctor regarding all test results. No news is not necessarily good news; it could mean system failure. I still give this advice to people today.

We did have some rare problems with our physicians. Once, one of our utilization management nurses was reviewing a patient's chart at one of our hospitals. The patient had been admitted for abdominal pain, and the patient's X-ray report stated the patient had a pneumoperitoneum. She noted the family practice physician had written a note on the chart stating that a surgeon had been called for a next-day appointment. But free air in the abdomen is considered a surgical emergency; the most common cause is a perforation or rupture in the stomach or bowel. Patients who have free air in their abdomen cannot afford to wait a day for a surgeon to evaluate them. The nurse called our office, and I called the medical director. He responded immediately and took control of the situation. He was a team player; the door to his office was always open for the quality nurses. This was a vast improvement from having multiple conflicts with physicians in my earlier nursing days. All physicians should know free air in the abdomen is an emergency and needs immediate further evaluation. The doctor who had arranged the next-day appointment would be contacted by the risk management committee about this case.

The quality nurses also performed random audits for quality markers established by the medical group (most were based on national treatment guidelines) such as adequate management of high blood pressure and annual eye examinations for diabetic patients. If a physician did not consistently meet quality markers he was sent a letter informing him and reminding him this was a goal of the organization.

I had been working for the company for a few years when the attorney asked me to review her notes on a pending case to see if I had anything to add about the patient's medical treatment. I took the papers home to review and returned them the next morning. I was promptly called back into her office. She asked me if I had been eating Cheetos while I was looking over the papers. I had, and I was absolutely mortified that I had been so careless and unprofessional Chalk it up as another life lesson for me!

We regularly surveyed the nine offices for cleanliness and appropriate monitoring of sterilizers and equipment, and we provided some staff education, as needed. I have no idea if or how this is done in private doctor's offices today. I'm bothered by the general lack of registered nurses in doctor's offices. I'm told hiring RNs is a cost-saving measure, but I wonder who teaches the medical assistants the basics of microbiology and the importance of properly cleaning equipment and monitoring sterilizers for medical instruments. My medical group employed RNs in all their offices.

I sat on a pharmacy committee which met monthly while working for the medical group. It was very enlightening. The committee, of course, tried to steer the physicians to order generic drugs rather than proprietary medications; but a mechanism was in place by which any physician could order the branded version of a drug if a patient did not seem to be responding to the generic formulation. The cost savings was huge, sometimes hundreds of thousands of dollars for an individual drug used by the company over the course of a year. Initially, I had the misconception that most of the HMO's pharmacy-related costs were generated by patients with conditions like AIDS, other cancers, or chronic diseases like multiple sclerosis. In fact, that was not the case. Instead, drugs to treat gastrointestinal-related conditions, the medications half of America seemed to take for their stomach complaints, generated the greatest pharmaceutical cost to the medical group. I thought this was in part because no one ever talked about the potential role of diet as a contributor to the national epidemic of acid reflux. Another large cost generator was a new category of psychiatric drugs to treat depression; these drugs were known as SSRIs (selective serotonin uptake inhibitors—think Prozac and Zoloft). SSRIs cost a fortune, until their patents expired and their generic versions became available. Today, the generic versions of some of these drugs cost as little as $4.00 for a thirty-day supply. A third costly category was the new allergy drugs which did not make patients drowsy, which once again became affordable—and were even available over-the-counter—after their patents expired. A pharmacist always sat on the committee and provided data about drug categories and drugs that could serve as potential substitutes for more costly formulations.

When the company attorney left the medical group, the quality improvement nurses took over some of her duties. The medical group used outside attorneys to handle potential and pending litigation. When I became involved in the process, there were fewer than fifteen cases for a member population of 90,000, which I think says a lot about the quality of the care we provided. I once sat with the junior attorney from the contracted firm, and it quickly became apparent he had very limited medical knowledge.

We were reviewing a complaint concerning a delay in the diagnosis of a patient's breast cancer. The patient had presented to the doctor with a small lump in her breast; the mammogram was negative, so the patient was told she did not need to do anything. At the next mammogram the lump was seen to have enlarged; the patient was sent to a surgeon and underwent biopsy of her breast, which revealed breast cancer. The junior attorney told me he had an expert witness who would testify that the doctor could tell whether a lump was cancerous by the feel of it during a breast exam. I almost fell out of my chair. No one can tell whether a lump is cancerous without a biopsy! The patient should have been sent to a surgeon after the first mammogram, to determine whether the lump in her breast was a fluid-filled cyst or a solid mass. A solid mass should be biopsied; that is the standard of care. I could unequivocally state this, because years earlier I had a lump in my breast, and I had gone through the process and underwent a biopsy.

No, we are not perfect, and we dropped the ball on this one. The medical group brought in a surgeon to offer a class to the physicians about the diagnosis and treatment of breast lumps. The QI nurses usually tried to attend physician-training sessions. We acted as the hostesses, too, arranging the chairs and making trips to the local supermarket for sandwiches. Why does it seem like woman's work spills into all facets of life? It wasn't a requirement of the job; it was just something we did. The surgeon gave a good class; he was funny and humble, too. He introduced himself as an expert, and said, by definition, that an expert is someone from out of town with slides (this was still during the days before PowerPoint).

Probably one of the most jaw-dropping experiences I had happened while I sat at the conference table listening to a discussion about a settlement package that was being prepared for a wrongful death lawsuit. Keep in mind: sometimes a case is settled even when wrongdoing on the defendant's part is not clear-cut. Medical malpractice suits can drag on for years, incurring a very high price tag on both the plaintiff and the defendant, to say nothing of the emotional toll taken on everyone involved. The financial settlement in a wrongful death lawsuit is calculated based upon the age, gender, education, and earnings potential of the deceased. This is common practice in the medical legal arena. I had no idea this process went on: placing a varying monetary price tag on human beings. I still can't process it very well, so maybe I'm not as hardened as I thought I was. What is the value of a housewife, or stay-at-home mother?

After four years the word was out that the insurance company that hired our medical group was getting out of the health care business. The medical group had also been sold; we were not certain there was any future. The resignations started, and no one was replaced. The secretaries started gossiping that the company was having difficulty making payroll. My father had experienced the same thing at one of his previous jobs. In his case, there was a buyout, and his company eventually closed shop. The employees who stayed to the very end never got paid.

I decided to leave my job. It had been a great experience, and I had made some good friends. But with a countless number of empty seats in the office, the handwriting was on the wall.

CHAPTER TWENTY

Rent-a-Nurse

———◆———

I joined a nursing agency and accepted a two-day office job, which was quite an eye-opener. I reported to the office of an endocrinologist, where my assignment was to provide IV medications for patients with multiple sclerosis and cancer. The regular nurse was going on medical leave. The doctor needed an RN, because medical assistants could not legally administer IV drugs; it was a state law.The office had a designated room where patients sat to receive their IV medication over a specified period, usually a half an hour. The room had two lounge chairs. The doctor regularly scheduled over 40 patients in one day, sometimes 50 were on the schedule. *Unbelievable, what kind of attention can you give a patient in, literally, just a few minutes? How could he keep that many people straight and complete his documentation promptly and accurately?*

On my first day in the office, there was a line of patients waiting to receive their IV therapy. Some of the patients had a surgically implanted port just under the skin of their chest walls. The port was accessed with a needle that plugged into it. The other end of the needle was then connected to a plastic tube which in turn was connected to the bag of IV fluid. (Patients who frequently received IV medications sometimes developed scars in the veins of their hands and lower arms; using a port prevented this.) Accessing a port was accomplished through a sterile procedure: we put on gloves and a mask and scrupulously cleaned the site of the port before entering the port with the needle, and this took a bit of time. I worked as fast as I reasonably could, but I still could not keep up with the assembly line they had going. At about noon I went to the office manager and informed her I had not taken a break and wanted to have some lunch. She looked at me incredulously and said that the regular nurse ate her lunch in the treatment room while watching her patients. I told her that I wished to leave and would be gone less than a half an hour. She commented, in a very curt tone, "You know you'll only back yourself up." I informed her that she was free to contact the agency to ask for another nurse who could do the job at a speedier pace than I could. Then she backed off.

I was given a very cold shoulder when I returned from lunch. The next day it was the same thing: *move, move, move, the patients are waiting.* And then a medical assistant came in with a patient record. She handed it to me, asking for my signature. I asked what it was. Apparently, under direction from either the doctor or the office manager, she had inserted a small needle into a patient then injected medication intravenously, to alleviate the line of patients.

She wanted me to sign the patient record saying that I had given the medication. I refused. Then I addressed this issue with the office manager. The manager said that medical assistants could do this under the doctor's direction and under the privileges of his license. I told her the doctor should sign for the medication, and I would *not* sign.

I was appalled that this practice took place. Doctors make certain that nurses don't practice medicine. I think nurses should make certain medical assistants don't practice nursing. I would advise any patient in a doctor's office receiving IV medications to ask the person administering the medication if she (or he) is a licensed nurse.

I finished my contract assignment at the office and but vowed to never return. That's how much of an unpleasant experience it was.

CHAPTER TWENTY-ONE

Insurance Nurse

2000

My family needed health insurance, but part-time nursing contracts did not provide this. It was the new millennium—the internet was now the place to look for employment. One of the big insurance companies was relocating its regional office to our city and needed nurses immediately for their utilization management team. My previous experience working for the medical group was apparently desirable, because the insurance company I had applied to called me within a week after I submitted my application.

Utilization managers at insurance companies are nurses who monitor hospital stays to determine whether they are appropriate. They record the patient's diagnosis and pertinent laboratory or X-ray findings that support the need for the patient's hospitalization. The insurance company nurses and their counterparts employed by the hospitals used nationally recognized software programs to determine whether admission criteria were being met and the anticipated length of stay. If the patient's stay exceeded the length that was anticipated, the nurse at the hospital had to provide more clinical data to justify the continued stay. If the stay was not justified, the insurance company would issue a denial, meaning the stay would not be paid for.

I made and received calls and faxes from hospitals all day. I entered the data into another software program created by my company. If the patient data met my company's criteria for admission, I could approve a hospital day (or days). If the criteria were not met, I had to send the data to one of the company's medical directors, for review. Nurses could never deny a hospital day without a doctor's review and approval. I know there is a misconception among the public that some nurse or some insurance man denies hospital days or treatments, but this is simply not the case. Common sense would tell you that an insurance company would never assume the legal liability they would expose themselves to if a layperson or a nurse were making these decisions. I screened hospital admissions with a software program. The company had a full complement of medical doctors on staff who made treatment decisions when the request for a procedure or hospital stay was a shade of grey rather than black-and-white.

What the public doesn't understand is that when corporate America purchases the insurance plans they offer their employees, they specify what they want in their policy. They can (and do) request specific verbiage in the plans that limits mental health care coverage or even disallows payment for procedures and treatments such as gastric bypass surgery and fertility treatment, which are elective procedures and are very expensive. People called my company in outrage because they had been denied services, pointing the finger at us, but sometimes we have nothing to do with the denial of a service. The customer's plan had simply been purchased that way. I also noticed that some companies offered different renditions of the same health plan to different categories of employees. Specifically, the managers at a company might get vision care included at no extra charge while the hourly employees paid extra. The caste system was alive and well in corporate America, as far as health insurance was concerned.

One day, I was standing in a hallway outside of my assigned medical director's office. The front of the office was glass, and I could see he was on the phone, so I waited patiently. I was there to discuss a patient who did not exactly meet the criteria for a continued stay in the hospital. I could approve the day, but a supervisor randomly audited our work, and an inappropriate approval would go on my evaluation. I had not reached my one-year anniversary with the company, and I followed the rules. But I also had the right to argue with a medical director that a patient should be granted a continued stay. We usually communicated with our assigned medical director by email, but it had been twenty-four hours and he had not replied. I knew the medical directors were kept as busy as the nurses; sometimes the only way to get something done was to show up in person.

My medical director was middle-aged and wore a bad comb-over on the top of his head. He came off as arrogant and was known to ask for detailed clinical information, which sometimes had nothing to do with a bed-day approval. I thought it was a power play he used for intimidation. I always prepared before I visited his office.

The case that day concerned a woman who had a hysterectomy. The software recommended a two-day hospital stay for the patient unless, of course, there were complications, such as a fever, unresolved pain, or nausea. On day three, the patient was, in fact, nauseated and vomiting. The difficulty—the shade of grey— rested in the fact that she had been given a suppository for the nausea rather than IV medication. The continued stay guidelines stated that IV medication should be necessary before the stay was granted. The key word here was *guidelines,* and most physicians at the hospital believe they should be able to make the final judgment call; after all, they are the one seeing the patient. I agreed with the patient's personal doctor and thought the patient should stay. The medical director listened to my case and, without missing a beat, declared, "Day denied, vomiting is available at home!"

I had to prepare a letter of denial and call the hospital and the doctor to inform them about the denial. I didn't really care for this part of the job; fortunately, it did not happen often. Sometimes the doctor I called offered a few choice words in response to the denial. The company had a strict format for the letter, and of course I had to sign my name to it. I felt like the front man and was reminded of an old medical joke. What are the three biggest lies in medicine? The answer is: "This won't hurt much," "We got it all," and "Your insurance company will pay for it." I knew the hospital would appeal the denial and later send a mountain of documentation. The case would be reevaluated by the appeals and grievance department at our company. Up goes the cost of the case...over just one bed-day. The administrative cost associated with an appeal might just end up exceeding the cost of paying for the day!Eventually, it dawned on me that health insurance companies are spending incredible amounts of money on nursing salaries to guard their profit margins. There were hospital gatekeepers like me and a division of nurses who sat on a phone queue to review outpatient procedures like CAT scans, MRIs, and certain medical procedures. There was a division that handled behavioral health care, the modern name for mental health care. There was a division of nurses that handled appeals and grievances. There was a quality assurance department that intermittently tapped into our phone calls with customers to make certain we were "talking the talk." There were two full floors of employees, and most of them were nurses. I think tracking all these hospital admissions could be done with a computer and a simple model that uses standard deviation to evaluate performance. We had diagnosis codes and codes for surgical procedures. If you matched them up with the number of days a patient stayed in the hospital you could easily put together either a hospital performance profile or individual physician performance profile. There was even a simpler way to monitor hospital days—and no computer would be needed. Walk onto any medical or surgical floor and ask the head nurse the names of the doctors who "parked their patients." They always know. Track only the doctors who park their patients. Reduce reimbursement to doctors and hospitals that don't perform well.

My workstation was a cube, but the general office environment was nice. Windows lined one wall of the room where my cube was located, so there was plenty of natural light. My coworkers were mostly middle-aged women, the same as me. I liked the fact I didn't have to start work at seven A.M., and that I got to wear nice clothes instead of scrubs. I quickly made friends, and at break time a group of us met outside on a loading dock, where we could smoke and chat. We were frequently joined by an aged surgeon who was one of the medical directors. His face was wrinkled from his lifelong tobacco habit, and he had very yellow teeth. I wondered why he was not retired, and I asked. He volunteered he had to work for tax payments and alimony payments. He was funny, and we enjoyed his company.

My daily workload was huge. I was never fully caught up—and neither were any of my coworkers. Patient names were added to my task list throughout the day. The supervisors reminded us that we were salaried, and we were to stay until the work was done. Most of us left at our appointed time anyway, because we found that if we ever finished our work on a given day, they just increased the load. Some of the older women worked through lunch in a futile effort to keep up. I thought of the *I Love Lucy* episode where Lucy is working in a chocolate candy factory and the company regularly speeds up the conveyor belt that carries the unwrapped candy for her to wrap. She starts snatching up individual candies and plopping them in her mouth as they pass by on the belt, just so there would be fewer candies she needed to deal with.

The phone queue job was just as busy. The division of nurses in the queue did occasionally uncover a significant issue. They discovered that the company spent far more money paying monthly rental fees for wheelchairs than they would have spent just buying the chairs outright for the patients. What a cash cow for the medical equipment company!

There were moments when we shared giggles, too, though. I was visiting a friend who worked on a phone queue when someone muted a caller to share the caller's request with the surrounding nurses. The caller wanted the insurance company to pay for a swimming pool at their home for arthritis therapy. One of the more outspoken nurses said, "Transfer that call right over to me and I will deny it so fast it will make their head swim!" The nurse who had taken the call didn't have to review this request with a medical director: swimming pools were not listed in the company manual as covered medical equipment.

I had three different supervisors during the time I was employed with the insurance company, which was about a year. The company had the habit of changing my cube slot every couple of months, and they also swapped out our computers, which was always a hassle, because some files always got shuffled, or sometimes even lost. If they were so concerned about productivity, why did they do this?

I had to shake my head at this one. I was in a meeting in a small side room with several other nurses and a medical director. We were all on a conference call. We gave a weekly report on all patients who remained hospitalized beyond guidelines. The power suddenly went out. The supervisor left the room and returned with flashlights and told us to keep working. The phone then went dead, so we were told we could return to our desks. We heard that a power line had been cut by the construction crew working across the street. We sat at our desks for over an hour with no power—meaning no computer and no air-conditioning. Of course, none of the windows open in modern office buildings. It was the middle of summer, and the building was heating up. We were finally, and reluctantly, sent home early.

I shook my head at my new assignment, too. I was given the nonparticipating cases, also known as non-par cases, in a certain geographic area in Florida. That meant I had to monitor patients who were in hospitals that we did not have contracts with. If the patients were emergency admissions, my assignment was to call the utilization nurse at the hospital and strongly urge that the patient be discharged or transferred to a hospital with which we were contracted as soon as the patient was stable. Insurance companies cannot control charges if a contract wasn't in place; they were therefore quite anxious to get the patients out of nonparticipating facilities.

One of my nonparticipating cases was a victim from an auto accident who had both extensive orthopedic surgery and plastic surgery. My company wanted him moved to a participating facility ASAP. The plastic surgeon took time out of his day to call me and ask if there was any way the patient could stay at the surgeon's facility. He said he put a lot of effort into this patient and was afraid the patient's results might be compromised by transferring him to an unknown doctor at another hospital. He wanted to follow him to recovery. I presented the case to the medical director, who did allow an extra few days, but the patient was ultimately transferred according to policy.

There were glitches with this policy; doctors cannot practice at any hospital. They must apply for privileges and go through a credentialing process to practice at any hospital. Most doctors practiced at a few hospitals within a given city. A doctor might be under contract with our insurance company, but due to circumstances beyond his control, the hospital where he practiced might not be contracted. Now, if the patient wanted to undergo surgery with the doctor who performed surgery only at the nonparticipating hospital, the patient and the doctor had a problem. The doctor would probably lose the patient's business, because the patient would have to pay a large penalty for having surgery performed at the nonparticipating hospital. The patient's physician choices were being governed by their insurance policy.

The issue of nonparticipating facilities came up to bite one of my neighbors. She took great care to make certain her pediatrician was a preferred provider on her health plan during the enrollment period in October. Then, in January, her son broke his leg, and he was hospitalized. After discharge, follow-up was performed in the pediatrician's office. Then my neighbors received a huge bill indicating her son's treatment had been provided by a nonparticipating doctor—her pediatrician! What happened between October and

January is anybody's guess, but that family should not have been penalized. My neighbor had to make numerous phone calls over several months to settle the dispute.

She was short and plump with salt-and-pepper hair cut in a short style. She was one of my coworkers, a nurse and a former nun. She was usually very patient, but on this day, she was clearly annoyed. The problem was gender bias in health care. She expressed disgust that women seem to be denied additional days after surgery on their reproductive organs, but men were not when it involved their reproductive organs. She declared, "All days for men with surgery below the waist are automatically approved." We didn't ask what prompted her outburst; we knew she spoke the truth. And the truth of gender bias extends into other areas.

I thought back to my emergency room days and remembered a lady who returned to the ER after we had treated her some weeks earlier. She wanted to tell us she had come in with back pain, was told her X-rays were negative, and was sent home with some oral medication that didn't begin to touch her pain. She was subsequently diagnosed with two ruptured disks, and she had undergone surgery. I understood the lady's anger, but X-rays often do not give a clear picture of what is going on in a patient; that's why patients are told to follow-up and have other studies performed if their problem persists. However, I have observed that when a man and a woman come in complaining about the same medical issue, like severe back pain, the man is more likely to receive an injection of narcotics and a prescription for narcotic medications than the woman. I don't know of any study to support this, it is just my observation. In any case, I thanked the lady for following-up and passed her information along.

Profits were down, and the company was "reorganizing." The corporate medical director and other officers in the company were replaced. One day, we came to work and several of our medical directors were gone. The doctor with the bad comb-over was among them—no loss there—but so was the doctor with the yellow teeth, who was okay. Several nursing managers who had been with the company for years had their jobs eliminated. Some employees resigned, and others were notified their jobs had been eliminated. I calculated twenty-five nurses on my floor had departed since I had joined the company.

My supervisor asked if I wanted to change jobs and become what was called a discharge planner. My assignment had been changed several times already, which impacted my productivity. That was important, because the company constantly measured employees' productivity. I asked if I could just keep my current job. I learned later this was a big mistake in corporate America. When a supervisor asks you whether you would like to change jobs, they aren't really asking, they are *telling* you what to do.

Anyway, I joined the pink slip crowd, and I was devastated, even though many other employees had also been pink slipped. One of the remaining medical directors came to my desk and said to me, "I heard, and I have no idea what criteria they used." That made me feel a little better. The director of nursing at the insurance company called me a few days later and offered me another position on a phone queue, which I declined, mostly out of injured pride. I took my severance, which was generous, and moved on.

CHAPTER TWENTY-TWO

Nursing Home

A position for an infection control nurse was listed in the news-paper. I faxed my resume from the local Kinko's. The phone was ringing when I returned home.

The job was at a nursing home. I would also be the employer's health care nurse who provided state-required continuing educa-tion to the staff. I was oriented by the person currently holding the position; she was planning to retire. She was responsible for ensur-ing all employees had their annual TB tests and were offered the hepatitis B vaccination. The state required annual training classes on fire safety and patient's rights; participation in the classes had to be documented. Nothing was on a computer at the nursing home, and there were over fifty employees. It was 2002, and the retiring nurse kept all the required information on index cards. I was told

I could borrow the activity director's computer when she was not using it (she typed the weekly activity sheets and newsletter).

Perhaps I was a little hasty in taking this job; the environment quickly became depressing. I walked into work through a lobby and the same man was always sitting in a wheelchair near the door. He appeared to be young, maybe fifty years old, and had apparently had a stroke: one arm was limp. I cheerfully introduced myself when I started at the nursing home. He replied with a name then added he was waiting to die! As my workday progressed, the halls filled with elderly residents in wheelchairs. Most of them sat with drooped heads and did not talk. There was a slight odor of urine in the air, which I found disagreeable.

There was one very elderly lady who walked the halls up and down most of the day, *every* day. She was hard to miss. because she was constantly changing her clothes throughout the day. She mumbled nonsense as she walked. One morning when I came to work, I was informed she had been transferred to the hospital after she had socked the night nurse in the nose. I remembered one of my ICU coworkers who had a broken nose after she was clobbered by a confused patient. (Classes on self-defense had never been offered in nursing school!)

I introduced myself to the nursing assistants and told them when their mandatory training classes were scheduled. I sat in the conference room at the appointed time, waiting for them to arrive. Maybe a quarter of them showed up on any given day. They were too busy tending to their patients. I kept rescheduling, and eventually I had to offer evening sessions to accommodate everyone.

Most of the real caretakers called nursing assistants had very thick accents; many were immigrants from Africa. I was never told how or why so many people from Africa landed at this facility. Once, after I had completed general orientation to new hires, I spoke at length to one gentleman who was in the class. He had been a teacher in Kenya but did not have his paperwork in place to work as a teacher in our country. He had taken a job at the nursing home, bathing and changing the diapers of the elderly residents, because it was the only job he could find. He was dignified, well spoken, and had my deepest respect. He did not share why he left Africa, however.

Another one of my responsibilities was to help pass out medications if a nurse called in sick. I had no problem with this, until I realized the patients with drooped heads who did not speak also did not wear wristbands. I was told this was the preference of the owner of the facility, and that there were pictures of the residents inside their charts on the first page. However, the first time I was called upon to give out the medications, I found several of the patient's pictures were missing. *Now what?* I thought. *How do I ensure I'm giving the correct medication to the correct patient?* I was told to ask the nursing assistants!

There was a language barrier with many of the nursing assistants too. They were a transient group, for obvious reasons (pay being at the top of the list!). I did not know any of them by name on this day. I thought about our society's priorities. We paid outrageous sums to hair salons for cuts and color, for tickets to sporting events, for meals at trendy restaurants, but we refused to pay a decent wage for day care workers and nursing home caretakers. Why is this?

I finally did find a reliable person I could communicate with. I was able to complete the medication administration that day, but it wasn't easy.

I stayed late one day so I could use the activity director's computer. I wanted to at least enter the date of each employee's last TB test on a spreadsheet, so I could sort the spreadsheet by status to see who was deficient. TB tests were administered on the date-of-hire anniversaries and not at one specific time during the year, which made employees' status more problematic to track.

As I sat at the activity director's cramped desk, piled high with papers, I heard someone who was obviously confused, screaming. The air smelled like dirty diapers. Then I suddenly noticed a train of ants making their way up the leg of the desk, heading toward my arm. That was the last straw; I resigned the next morning, before I had even completed six weeks. The administrator and director of nurses were not pleased. I never looked back—nor put the experience on my resume.

CHAPTER TWENTY-THREE

Return to Hospital Nursing

In 2002 I went job-hunting again. What a low blow. My phone calls to the local hospitals were answered by people who informed me that because I had not worked in a hospital for more than two years they didn't want me unless I took a refresher course. I was taken aback and somewhat angry, because I thought my clinical knowledge was at an all-time high and that I would have no problem tackling any job. It wasn't as if I had been out of nursing for years; I had simply been working in a different capacity, from a desk. I could understand making someone return to school for a competency validation if they had not worked in any nursing job for years. Ultimately, I swallowed my pride and did what I was told.

I signed up at a local university for a nursing reentry program. I paid the $1,000 fee and headed to class. I can't say I learned

215

anything new. I met another nurse there who was in the same boat that I was. She had been a medical consultant and was told she did not have the skills to work in a hospital without a refresher course. The last day of class, the two of us completed our tests and were out the door while the rest of the class were scratching their heads and agonizing over answers. After the lectures and the successful testing, part two of the reentry program was a six-week internship in a hospital—with no pay.

We could request a specific hospital and area to work. The university would make the arrangements. My first thought was to return to the emergency department, because I had worked there the most during my career. I reported to the ER on the assigned day and met my preceptor. She worked twelve-hour shifts, and I would follow her schedule. I had worked a few double shifts for extra money when I was in my twenties but had never regularly worked twelve-hour shifts.

It was exhausting. I was on my feet most of the time. The paperwork appeared to have tripled since my last ER job. Also, I didn't like the new edict that nurses had to help patients out of cars; more than a few were big and heavy. The security guards at the hospital used to help patients out of cars, but now they were generally not available because of a reduced staff. On my third day, I had barely finished hanging up my coat when the squawk box said the helicopter was on the way with a victim from an auto accident. The patient arrived in a flurry of activity. He was unconscious and covered in blood. One of his lower legs was broken, and the bone had pierced through his skin.

I did not feel energized or important. I felt sad and tired. Later, I overheard one of the young nurses expressing excitement to another nurse about getting to see a leg that had a compound fracture. Could it be I should end my days in the ER? My decision was set in stone when I observed the group dynamics of the staff. The ER doctors acted distant; I had no sense of camaraderie between them and the nursing staff. There was also some ill will among the nurses themselves. I was told it all came down to salary.

Apparently, the emergency department had been having difficulty recruiting nurses and was forced to use agency nurses. Some of the agency nurses had been working at the facility for months and apparently were paid about 20 percent more than the hospital employees, resulting in more than a little acrimony. I overheard a vicious exchange one day between my preceptor and an agency nurse. One of them declared the other incompetent. The argument took place in front of several patients. I was embarrassed to even be there. I had never seen such a thing in all my years of nursing. Shortly after the argument, my preceptor went home. The charge nurse walked up to me and handed me the pile of charts for the patients my preceptor had been assigned. Then the charge nurse walked away.

I didn't even know where all the supplies were kept or what was required of the paperwork. I followed the charge nurse and said, as politely as I could, that I was on orientation and felt it was inappropriate to be handed a pile of patients with no directions. She wordlessly took the charts back and walked away again, leaving me on my own to orient myself.

That night I called the university contact and said I had made a mistake. I related what happened and asked to be assigned somewhere else, preferably somewhere that didn't require twelve-hour shifts. I was told there was an opening in the hospital's outpatient surgery department.

Patients reported to the outpatient surgery area on the day of their operation. The nurses ensured that all pre-op test results were on the patient's chart and that any abnormal test results were addressed. They checked the surgical consent form to make certain the type of surgery and the surgical site were identified correctly. Then the patients were instructed to put on a gown, and the nurses started them on an IV. If a patient was undergoing a joint replacement, the nurses scrubbed the surgical site.

My new coworkers were helpful and nice. They were no agency nurses; most of the staff had been there for years. There were two shifts in the department, an eight-hour day shift and an eight-hour evening shift. If an evening case was still in the department at eleven P.M., an "on-call" nurse would take over. I liked the hours and my new coworkers. At the end of my internship, I was offered a permanent job in the department, which I accepted. I recertified in advanced life support. I had not forgotten the meaning of the waveforms on the cardiac monitor, despite having worked at a desk for a few years.

I was asked to float to the recovery room to help cover "holes" in staffing. There I learned something new. Postoperative pain medications were given intravenously with pumps that the patients controlled themselves. The medications and their dosage were ordered by the anesthesiologists or the surgeons. The nurses drew up the drug and injected it into the bag of IV fluid; then the tubing was threaded through a pump. The nurses programmed the pump to deliver the proper dose when prompted by a control button pushed by the patient. This was a big win for the patients: they did not have to wait for a nurse to answer their call bell to be administered their pain medication or to receive it by way of an intramuscular shot. The pumps delivered a specified amount in a specified timeframe. After the patient reached the maximum amount of medication in the time frame the doctor prescribed, the pump just quit delivering. The patient could keep pushing the button but would not receive anything. It was the nurse's responsibility to assess the patient's pain level and keep the patient's doctor in the loop.

The nurses monitored and documented a patient's pain with a numeric value of 1 to 10, with 10 being the worst. If the nurse assessed the prescribed dose of pain medication was not sufficient, she contacted the doctor about increasing the dose. If the patient was excessively drowsy the nurse would contact the doctor to decrease the dose or maybe try an oral medication and take the patient off the intravenous medication. Patients with chronic back pain were often on narcotics for years just to allow them to perform activities of daily living; most had developed a tolerance to their medication, so they sometimes required a higher dose.

I was astounded to see how big the patients had become. The recovery room nurses routinely transported their patients to the floor if they were admitted after surgery. At times this was very difficult. The department finally hired a large assistant to help move patients on and off the OR table and transport them to the floor, which was a blessing.

The hospital had a contract with a company to provide bigger hospital beds for the large patients undergoing bariatric surgery (an operation that allows the patient to lose weight by shortening the patient's intestinal tract). But the hospital had been built decades earlier, so the doorways to the patient rooms barely allowed the bigger beds through (...and I mean *barely!*). One night, I was recovering a large lady after she had bariatric surgery. Because it was evening, the big assistant was at his home, so I had to find a coworker to help transfer my patient to the floor.

We struggled. The bed and the patient were very heavy; additionally, we had the pain pump to deal with. When we finally arrived at the doorway of the patient's room, there was some inevitable jostling—we couldn't get the bed through the door. The patient's husband was waiting in the hallway and began to cuss us out for bumping the doorjamb. We finally took the side rails off the bed to get it through the door. Of course, we apologized to the patient and her husband, even though the size of her bed and the width of the doorway were not our fault.

Another time, I prepared to discharge a young woman after she had an operation on one of her forearms. The arm was splinted and in a sling. I helped her to the bathroom, but she was so big that she was unable to reach far enough to pull her pants up or down with her good arm. I knew she was humiliated, and I truly felt for her.

Clearly, something is wrong with the food we are eating. I can't believe so many people are unable to control their weight. Even one of our general surgeons was more than a little overweight. One of the nurses made up a song about him (this was *not* the most professional behavior, but we did change the name in the song, so no one would know who we were referring to). We thought he was arrogant and crabby, so one day, in the privacy of a storage room, we all had a guiltless laugh over the song.

Rush, rush seemed to be the mode of operation in the OR and the recovery room. We had to keep to the schedule. This caused some friction between the OR staff members and the recovery room nurses.

The recovery room nurses were annoyed when patients were transferred from the OR with a nonfunctioning IV or a wet gown. The IV should have been addressed, and the patient should have been cleaned up before leaving the OR table. The staff managing the patient's anesthesia occasionally pulled the endotracheal tube too soon, in which case the recovery room nurse would have to manually hold the patient's jaw in the correct position to keep the airway open to facilitate breathing. I even noticed a few people not consistently wiping the rubber port on the plastic IV tubing with an alcohol swab before administering an IV medication. Having previously been an infection control nurse, I had to comment on this oversight to the people who skipped the step.

I was also sometimes troubled by the general cleanliness (or lack thereof) of the recovery room. When we started our days I

sometimes found that the recovery room's main sink and coun-
tertops had not been cleaned overnight and were visibly dirty.
Housekeeping did not "get to us" until later in the morning. We
had a utility room where soiled equipment was dropped off before
it was cleaned and reprocessed. The room needed more frequent
cleaning than it received. I would always pick up the phone and
complain to the housekeeping department. I told my supervisor
what I observed, and she agreed, but nothing ever really changed.

So? Do you think *rush, rush* and cuts in housekeeping staff
could have something to do with hospital acquired infections?

Despite some cleanliness deficiencies, the hospitals did take surgical errors seriously and worked very hard to prevent them. We
made certain we had the right patient, the right surgery, and the
right site. On some patients, the nurses marked the surgical site in
washable ink. The patient's allergies were listed on the front of the
patient chart in addition to being identified on the patient's allergy
armband. Most of the operations went off without a hitch, and I
was happy to see there were people who went over and beyond the
call of duty to make sure patients were safe.

I had had an exhausting day. Plus, I was chastised for being tactless.

The nurses in the recovery room started work at seven A.M.
Now it was around one P.M. Most of us had not had lunch—including me. I made a comment about it to one of my coworkers in
earshot of the doctors and was called on it by the supervisor. She

informed me complaints were not to be made out in the open, and she reminded me that I was a nurse. I should eat crackers if I was hungry she said: we always kept saltines in the recovery room for nauseated patients.

I had complained because I knew the anesthesiologists NEVER missed lunch. My teenage son laughed out loud when I told him the story about the crackers. In her defense, the supervisor tried to get us some help after our discussion to ensure we could manage to eat our lunches; she even bought sandwiches on some days when we were too busy to leave the department.

I was preparing an elderly gentleman for surgery: an amputation of a toe for gangrene associated with his diabetes. I pricked his finger to perform a blood sugar test before the operation. His fasting blood sugar level was abnormally high at 175 milligrams per deciliter. Medical research has proven that consistently high blood sugar levels are associated with circulation problems as well as eye and kidney damage. At this point in my career I had learned something about tact, so I treaded lightly after I informed the patient of his number. I asked him what he and his family doctor had decided was a "good" number for him. He answered without a pause, "Right about there; it's where I feel best!" I could give the doctor the benefit of the doubt and assume the patient misunderstood his treatment, but I had heard the same story from other patients involving several different doctors over the years.

Fortunately, the health insurance companies have taken steps to improve diabetes care these days. Once they figured out the huge dent diabetes was making to their bottom line, they hired nurses to call patients and offer diabetes health care training over the phone. They also started monitoring the quality of care provided to diabetic patients at doctors' private offices. Nurses were hired to go into the offices and record patient blood sugar levels and physicians' treatment plans. The insurance company also wanted to ensure that a hemoglobin A1C test had been performed on patients with diabetes. This test determines the patient's average blood sugar level over a three-month period. They were also looking for documentation of health education at the office and documentation that recommendations for regular eye exams had been made to the patients. Doctors can't control a patient's compliance at home, but they can make recommendations. Some of the doctors didn't like being audited, but it was part of their contract with the health insurance company, so they had no choice. Doctors not following national guidelines could receive a letter from the insurance company reminding them of the national standards for the treatment of patients with diabetes.

Over the years I had learned not only tact but also how to better communicate my opinion to prevent a confrontation with a physician.

Once, when I walked into my patient's room in the outpatient surgery department to provide discharge instructions, I saw the front of the man's pants was soaked with blood. His operation was called a cystoscopy, which was an examination of his bladder with a catheter that has a lens and that goes through the patient's penis. I asked the patient to lie down then grabbed a towel. His blood pressure and pulse were fine, so I picked up the phone and paged the urologist. He answered and told me to put in a catheter. I said, "No, I think you should check him and put in the catheter, there may be swelling." He paused briefly and then reluctantly agreed to return.

The point was that I had no idea what was causing the bleeding from the patient's urinary tract, and because the urologist had just recently been looking around in the patient's bladder, *he* needed to deal with it. If something was amiss, I didn't want to be blamed for performing a traumatic catheterization. I had learned to cover myself. My coworkers stood solidly behind me on this one.

Later that day, one of my coworkers relayed a story from the previous evening. Her patient underwent a gallbladder removal with a scope and was supposed to be discharged to her home, but the patient's blood pressure after the operation was lower than her baseline blood pressure, and her heart rate was high, over 100 beats per minute. She said she was not comfortable sending the patient home and called the surgeon. He gave her no end of grief, but she stood her ground, adamant that he needed to come in and look at the patient. She had been a nurse for over thirty years and was comfortable questioning the patient's status. The surgeon did come in, and the patient was admitted overnight to receive IV fluids.

Paying attention to patient's vital signs was Nursing 101. Healthy people do not have heart rates over 100 beats per minute when they are at rest. That high of a heart rate means the patient is in pain, or something else is wrong.

It was midnight, and I was on my way to the recovery room. I was the nurse on call that night, and although I had to be on call only twice a month, I did not like this obligation, because I was *always* called. Usually things went smoothly, and I rarely had more than one patient, but on this night there were back-to-back emergencies. I pushed my last patient to the floor after three-thirty A.M. I was so tired that I was afraid to drive home. There wasn't a full-sized sofa in the lounge, so I pushed several chairs together and sprawled across them, using my winter coat as a cover. I wasn't the only one who had this problem. One of the other nurses told me she had to stop in a Walmart parking lot one morning to nap, because she was too tired to make it home. Everyone hated being on call except for one of our part-time nurses who worked as a drug salesman during the day. He liked being on call because of the money. He was young, and I was sure he was not the one getting up with the kids or getting them off to school in the morning, like most of us.

On my next call night, I had only one patient and was ready to go by one A.M. I walked through the emergency room, but before I went outside, I realized there was some sort of disturbance in the parking lot, arising from a group of young men. I thought it might be best to wait for security. I was parked in the hospital's surface lot, but quite a distance out. I was ever-mindful of the poor lab tech at one of the places I worked who had been raped in the parking garage after she had left work at night alone. When I regularly worked the second shift, the nurses always left together.

I called security and was told someone would come by shortly. A half an hour later, I called again—and then again. No one picked up the phone after my first call. It is a shame that nurses are unable to obtain basic security service. We had been told during our hospital orientation that security would always be available for the nurses. What a laugh.

The men causing the disturbance finally disappeared, and one of the women who worked in the admissions office walked with me to my car, so I could finally head home.

I had another challenge being on call: I had to learn to communicate with patients who did not speak English. This was not an insignificant issue, because we were seeing a significant number of Hispanic patients at our hospital. They lived in a cluster of apartments near the hospital. Many were laborers working in the home-building business. In fact, I regularly saw a dozen or more men dressed in jeans and work overalls on a certain street corner I passed on the way to work. Sometimes I saw a pick-up truck come by: the men climbed in the open back. Supposedly, more than a few of them were in the country illegally; I'm certain they were paid far less than union wages. I had to learn a few words and phrases in Spanish: "Sir, your operation is over, and you are doing well." "Take a deep breath." "Do you have pain?" "Where is your pain?"

Regardless of their immigration status, I believed these people were decent, hard workers.

One night, I was managing the recovery of a man who had undergone an emergency appendectomy. His brother came in and immediately asked when he would be able to return to work. The patient asked the same thing after he awakened from his anesthesia. Another night, I managed the recovery of a man who had undergone brain surgery to relieve a clot after falling off a roof. He had no health insurance and would probably be in the hospital for weeks. Construction workers illegally in our country with no insurance was a significant problem for hospitals and part of the reason patients with insurance see outrageous charges for items like splints and aspirin. The hospitals inflated charges to make up for those who didn't pay. Some people think those patients should be denied care. But how do you deny care to someone who is in a life-threatening situation? How do you deny medical assistance to a pregnant woman ready to deliver her baby? You can't.

My job also included working in the hospital's preoperative area. Here we obtained the patient's health history and drew blood for lab tests. We sent the patients for chest X-rays and performed EKGs according to a protocol based on the patient's age and known health conditions. Patients scheduled for joint replacement surgery saw a physical therapist and received a brief explanation of what to expect after surgery.

I saw the same clinical picture over and over. There were so many overweight people on a lot of medications for conditions most certainly associated with their weight. All patients had to be weighed before anesthesia so the dosage of their medication could be accurately calculated. Some of the patients weighed more than the scale could display, in which case we relied on the patient's estimation. I could tell they were incredibly embarrassed when this happened. Also, a significant number of patients did not know the names of all their medications. We told them to type up a list and carry it with them in their wallets. (It is *so* important to know your medications, not only to reduce the chances that you'll experience complications during or after your operation, but also in case you ever need to be treated in an ER.) The number of medications a typical patient was on had probably tripled since I had first become a nurse, although I have never seen any hard data on this subject, nor any correlation between the quantity of medications and a patient's quality of life. Many medications had similar names, and we constantly referred to our pharmaceutical reference book to sort things out. Maybe the sheer number of medications—along with the confusing names of their generic formulations—made the patients give up control. I noticed the patients referred to their medications by color and size. They would say things like "I take the blue one in the morning and two white ones at noon." They seemed to have no grasp of the possible side effects, so the nurses tried to review this issue with them, if it was pertinent. Alternatively, we encouraged them to review all their medications the next time they visited their doctor. We also advised patients to ask for copies of results from diagnostic tests like EKGs or lung tests. Tests are unnecessarily repeated, because we are unable to obtain copies of any previous results from doctor's offices. Some days we just didn't have time to call offices—and when we did, we sat on hold. Tests are *very* expensive, and unnecessary repetition was part of the underlying reasons behind rising health care costs.

A patient came in for a hernia repair. He was having his pre-op work performed on the day of surgery, which is sometimes done when the operation is considered minor. As soon as he walked in, he grabbed a trash can and started throwing up. I called over to surgery to let the surgeon know that it looked like the surgery might need to be postponed to another day. The surgeon came right over to pre-op, because he still wanted to take the patient into surgery. The patient's head was in the trash can when the surgeon arrived. He could not stop heaving. I gave the surgeon the dirtiest look I could conjure— and finally he then canceled the operation.

My next patient was one of the supervisors from the insurance company that had laid me off. She recognized me and immediately said there were open positions. I said no thanks and tried not to give her the dirty look, too.

I continued to learn important lessons from my patients, even after all my years as a nurse. They told stories about what had and had not worked for them. They relayed how their diseases affected their lives and what they did to manage on a day-to-day basis. While some diseases are most certainly related to poor lifestyle choices, there is no question some people were dealt a bad hand at birth. I truly sympathized with the patients with neurologic diseases that left them immobile, or the patients with lung disease like cystic fibrosis. We saw numerous patients with chronic back pain. Many of them had had multiple operations or repeated physical therapy stints and *still* had to take daily narcotics to function. I hated so see patients who were plagued with serious post-op infections after a routine operation. Some of them were young and healthy and had no risk factors for infection, like diabetes. They had to be administered antibiotics intravenously for weeks, or even months. I thought all hospitals should be required to post their infection rates. There are better business bureaus and *Consumer Reports* to check before we buy goods or services...but there's nothing to check regarding individual hospital and doctor infection rates.

One of the more positive aspects of this hospital was its staff of dedicated volunteers. They were mostly retired seniors—and they were a pleasure to work with. They were punctual and good humored. They ran specimens to the lab, called back patients from the waiting room, made up beds, and looked for lost wheelchairs. There was one retired businessman I particularly enjoyed working with. He shared stock tips with the nurses, along with his take on modern life. He said, "King-sized beds are too big. By the time I find my wife I've forgotten what I'm supposed to do."

CHAPTER TWENTY-FOUR

Case Manager

2007

I received a large postcard in the mail for a job fair hosted by another health insurance company and decided to see what they were offering. They offered a better commute and better pay. The job was different than the one I had previously held. My title was case manager.

My cube was in a high-rise with beautiful views. The grounds around the office complex had walking paths, landscaped with fountains and flowers—a welcome change from the asphalt parking lots of the hospital.

The RN case manager service was an extra charge on health insurance plans sold to employers. Companies purchased it in hopes of saving money. The insurance company's computer identified members with chronic diseases or a high utilization profile;

in other words, patients who generated the most cost based on their claims.

Hospital admission generated huge costs. The names and phone numbers of members who were admitted to a hospital were forwarded to the nursing staff for intervention. Companies became creative in trying to identify high risk patients who had not been hospitalized. Some made it mandatory for their employees to fill out a health assessment as part of their insurance coverage. Other companies raffled off electronics, like big screen TVs, to employees who filled out a health assessment. I wondered just exactly who had access to our data and if a line was ever crossed that should have protected patients under the health privacy act known as HIPAA (Health Insurance Portability and Accountability Act), which is legislation enacted in 1996 to protect patients' privacy.

I also came to realize that claims data did not always paint an accurate picture of reality. A nurse friend of mine shared that she was contacted by a case manager from her insurance company to discuss her chronic obstructive pulmonary disease (COPD). She was asked how long she had smoked. My friend was shocked: she had never been diagnosed with COPD...and she had never smoked. She had mistakenly been labeled as a patient with COPD because she had been prescribed an inhaler for temporary use after a prolonged bout of bronchitis the previous winter.

After I reviewed my daily assignment, which I could bring up on my computer, I made phone calls to the members. Our objective was to offer health care information, then encourage our members to enroll in classes for chronic problems like asthma, COPD, or diabetes, if applicable; the classes were conducted over the phone. If they had had a recent hospital admission, we asked if a follow-up appointment had been scheduled with their doctor, and we reviewed their medications. We also mailed out educational materials.

There was a script to follow for our calls. If a patient was interested in our help, we would set up a health improvement goal with them and make follow-up calls to check on their progress. The objective was to encourage healthful habits, including medication compliance, and thus reduce hospital admissions and costs.

It was not a bad idea, in theory, but there were days when I reached only two or three patients. The rest of my time was spent leaving voice messages and documenting that I had called and left a message. Sometimes I spent a significant amount of time looking for the phone numbers of my assigned members, if the number I had been provided proved invalid. Members obviously did not want to share their phone numbers; otherwise, they would have listed it on their forms. We were required to make three attempts to reach members before a case could be closed.

I realized there could be a reason for the difficulty reaching patients identified for case management. Data entry of members' claims was outsourced and some of the companies were located outside of the United States. This caused a delay in getting members' health care status into our system. For example, a member might have been hospitalized for a heart attack, but the case manager might not receive the case until three months after the fact, when the member was already back at work and wasn't home to answer our call. As a result, some of the folks I spoke with told me they had no health issues or questions then hung up, contrary to what the computer profile indicated about them. I did somewhat understand the members' response: I was making a cold call, and sometimes people just don't want to talk about private health issues on the telephone with a stranger.

That said, some patients were lonely and grateful to share the daily trials and tribulations associated with their health conditions, particularly those with chronic pain, and they always answered the phone. Other patients stopped answering phone calls after one or two sessions. All the nurses had to submit a monthly written patient "success story" to our supervisor. Some months I had to count a small success with a patient, like they kept a follow-up appointment or finally understood their blood pressure numbers.

It was disconcerting to recite the verbiage prepared for us for our phone calls and not have the power to follow through. At the beginning of my calls, I spouted, "I am here to help you with your health questions and needs." But I was sometimes not able to help, despite being an insider. A case in point was a patient who bought a wig after losing her hair to chemotherapy. Her health insurance policy said the wig was a covered expense, but she never received reimbursement. When I made calls for her to find out why, my experience was the same as that of the patient: I sat on hold, was transferred numerous times, and was finally told that the patient's reimbursement request did not have the proper code. But when I asked, no one could give me the proper code. Hair loss from chemotherapy to treat breast cancer is not that unusual. It was discouraging to see this type of disconnect at a national company, and I reported it to my supervisor. I thought, *Don't sell what you can't deliver* but I kept my thoughts to myself.

I heard more than a few legitimate customer service complaints from patients. Sometimes their mail order prescription renewals did not arrive on time. This was particularly upsetting to the patients who had diabetes. Then they were unable to speak to a real person on the phone at the mail order pharmaceutical company: they just went around in circles pressing phone prompts or put on hold. Some days I spent a fair amount of time pressing the same phone prompts, trying to help them.

I spent hours trying to expedite the process for obtaining a new wheelchair for a child. He had grown considerably over the previous two years, but our company would not accept any phone information from the boy's parents about his current height and weight. The guidelines stated he needed to be reevaluated by a physical therapist before he could be reimbursed for a new chair. Unfortunately, he lived in rural America. The only company available under his plan that could provide a physical therapy consult had staffing issues and the member had to wait for months before he could be seen. My efforts to expedite the process were unsuccessful.

Some things had not changed since I was last employed in the insurance industry. Health insurance policies were sold in many renditions and customer service had to scroll through online binders to determine what was covered. This is very time consuming. Certain plans dictated which specialists a patient could see and where the patient could obtain services, such as an X-ray or lab work. Patients might be expected to travel up to twenty-five miles from their home to obtain service from a contracted company. This was a true hardship on many families and many patients, particularly the elderly, if the commute passed through a metropolitan area with traffic issues.

The phone number for the nurse's queue was printed on the back of each patient's health card. Some patients called to complain about customer service delays and the poor availability of providers. They hoped to get a more expeditious answer from a nurse, but we were told not to quote benefits, and of course we couldn't change contract terms or enlarge the panel of doctors who accepted their insurance.

The insurance company monitored everything we did. We were placed on the phone queue, which was not part of the job when I accepted it. I had to sign out for any breaks I took, including all bathroom breaks, as well as lunch. Of course, the company had software that counted our calls and determined how long we were on each call. We received intermittent report cards on how we performed compared to our other team members. One day, an instant message from my supervisor appeared on my computer screen, asking what I was doing since I hadn't made a call in almost fifteen minutes. I was a little incensed, because my productivity had always been good. I was doing internet research on an unusual disease before making a call to the patient. I thought it was important to be knowledgeable before talking with the patient. As a seasoned professional I thought the company's monitoring practices were kindergarten stuff, but I kept my opinion to myself.

I spoke to many early retirees who expressed shock about monthly premiums over $900 (unfortunately a reasonable rate in today's market) to cover themselves and their spouses. The amount was more than their mortgages. Some had worked for nationally known companies for decades. They said they had accepted an early retirement because they knew they otherwise would be laid off. They had no idea their option to purchase healthcare with the company would come with such a high price tag. Many of them were unable to shop around for another insurance carrier at the time because they had preexisting conditions. One gentleman told me "HMO" meant "'healthy members only." Cardiac medications and supplies to help patients with diabetes cost hundreds of dollars per month, and insurance companies used the preexisting loophole whenever possible to dodge patients who needed these items. By far the most egregious story I've heard regarding denial of coverage for a preexisting condition came from a friend. She fell while skiing and broke her hip. Her health insurance at the time was a COBRA policy, which she had taken out following a divorce. The policy expired before she had fully recovered. When she attempted to purchase another policy with the same company, she was told her hip was a preexisting condition, so physical therapy would not be covered. The insurance companies always paid better than the hospitals, but my job satisfaction was marginal.

In 2011 I tried another case management position, where I dealt exclusively with Medicaid patients. The job had the same objectives as the previous one: educate the members on how to better manage their health and keep them out of the hospital. These members were easier to reach than those on commercial insurance (most were unemployed) but more challenging to communicate with because of their educational background. A significant number of them had not completed high school. Some were limited in the length of time they could talk each month, because only 250 minutes of phone time was provided on their government-sponsored phone plan. The allotted minutes were used up quickly by waiting on phone queues, trying to reach overwhelmed medical offices on their Medicaid plan, or to arrange rides to get there. I personally experienced frustrating wait times trying to reach a physician or a pharmacist to resolve a prescription or medical equipment issue. At the end of the month, when calls were answered with a message stating that the phone was out of service, we knew to retry on the first of the month, when minutes would be added to phone plans.

Our company had contracts with one of the large teaching hospitals located in the city. It had a great reputation and offered specialty clinics in internal medicine, endocrinology, cardiology, pulmonology, and psychiatry. However, the clinics were staffed by rotating residents, and our members frequently saw so many specialists they could not remember the doctors' names or specialty, much less what they were told about their condition. Consequently, I did derive a sense of purpose and accomplishment explaining the patients' health problems and treatment in terms they could understand.

Additionally, all the nurses were assigned an assistant, someone called a "navigator," who personally visited the members monthly in their homes. The members could identify an actual face for the company. Navigators ensured the members had all the medical equipment they needed, and they helped facilitate transportation. They also reported back to their assigned nurse whether they had noted safety issues or lack of food in a home. Sometimes, when I was unable to reach a member, the navigator knocked on the member's door. If the member answered, she put them on the phone to talk with me. I liked the navigator business model and thought it helped a lot with member compliance.

The nurses made a few home visits every month to those patients with the most health-related issues. They wanted to determine if we could impact these patients' health habits with face-to-face advice. Despite public perception about the welfare system being a "giveaway" by the government, some of the patients I visited lived in tiny spaces in run-down buildings. My navigator reported seeing roaches and broken plumbing. I had a middle-aged woman on disability for schizophrenia that called me regularly and talked nonsense when she skipped her medications. When I visited her at her home, I found she shared her check—and her studio apartment—with her daughter and her daughter's boyfriend. They used a shopping cart they had taken from some local grocery store as a dresser in the living room. The daughter and the boyfriend were about twenty years old; both were dropouts and unemployed. The boyfriend sat playing games on his smart phone while I was there. No explanation was offered for their situation.

There was a high incidence of mental health problems among the Medicaid patients. It was unclear to me whether poverty caused mental health problems or untreated mental health problems caused poverty. I learned a lot about the state of the mental health care industry today, and it is a bit distressing. The biggest issue is the wait time for patients to get an appointment with a psychiatrist; sometimes it takes months. While the patient is waiting to get an appointment, prescriptions run out if the member does not have the foresight to schedule an appointment before the prescription expires. I was told there is currently a shortage of psychiatrists. Family doctors can and do write prescriptions for medications to treat depression, but some of the members I worked with required more than a single medication to treat their condition and needed to see a psychiatrist who was more familiar with simultaneously prescribing multiple medications to treat a single behavioral health issue. Psychiatrists could provide talk therapy—meaning counseling—but many did not; it seemed that medication management had become their primary function. People don't lie on couches in psychiatrist's offices and have their minds "probed" like in the old movies or on TV. Patients must make another appointment to see someone else.

Psychologists diagnose and treat mental disorders but can't write prescriptions because a psychologist with a PhD in psychology is not the same as a medical doctor. I thought that psychologists did most of the counseling, but that had changed, too. Counselors and therapists did most of the face-to-face interactions with my members in the Medicaid population; I was told psychologists did tests.

The role of counselor versus therapist was confusing to me, so I asked at work and looked it up on the internet. A few sites said counselors offered guidance to people to deal with mental conflicts and interpersonal behavior; their educational background was varied, and they might not have a professional license. Therapists generally had a master's degree and taught people ways of coping with their feelings and situations. Then there were mental health technicians, who worked in hospitals and institutions. "Techs" were trained on the job or had a certificate or associate degree. They monitored patient behavior, administered medications, and helped with activity groups. There seemed to be potential for fragmentation of care—and I remained confused.

In addition to not being sure who is who in the mental health arena, I was taken aback at what I believed were stingy inpatient stays. I followed a man admitted from an outpatient treatment home because he threatened violence and refused to wear clothing. He was an inpatient for forty-eight hours, then went back to the home, only to be readmitted over and over for the same problem. Patients who expressed thoughts of suicide also seemed to be discharged rather quickly. They were given instructions to follow up their care at an outpatient setting. I wondered if everyone made it.

The Medicaid job was my first real prolonged encounter with the poor. I thought it was unacceptable to see so many children born into poverty. I couldn't understand why people weren't using birth control when they couldn't even pay their utility bills. Condoms were free on our medical supply list. One of my coworkers mentioned at a team meeting that the poor don't seem to want to use them. *How do you get or keep a job when you never finished high school and keep having babies? Is there a monetary benefit from the government for having multiple children?* I voiced my disgust at work one day and was given a thought-provoking retort by the social worker. She said, "Poor people want children too." I still think society should instill the concept of personal responsibility and women should not be having children with multiple men who become absent fathers.

A few months later the same social worker came to the office upset and indignant. She had given a member a voucher, allowing her to purchase a roomful of furniture at the city furniture bank for $40. The member called her back and chewed her out about the poor selection!

Like my previous insurance work, everything was monitored and analyzed, but at this job we were given feedback telling us that the hospital admission rate among our Medicaid members had decreased, and that the lower rate was attributable to case management, which was very encouraging. We also counted our successes at our team meetings. The company had quarterly meetings which offered a company update and staff education followed by a nice luncheon. My last employment experience was very positive.

CHAPTER TWENTY-FIVE

Retirement

I left my Medicaid case manager position and retired to the sunshine. But after a year I decided to take one last contract job—a job that allowed me to work from home. I was part of an auditing team performing a project known as HEDIS (Health Effectiveness Data and Information Set). HEDIS data is collected annually by all the major health plans. The data measure the performance of the health plan regarding the management of a variety of health conditions. For example, we reviewed medical records to record the blood pressures of members who were receiving treatment for a diagnosis of hypertension. The goal was to find documentation of a blood pressure within the normal range after treatment. We recorded the A1C test results indicating average blood sugars for diabetic members. We recorded the number of children who completed their immunizations and the number of women who had Pap smears and mammograms in the recommended time-frame. There were multiple other measures we recorded, and some changed annually. The measures were determined by the National Committee for Quality Assurance. Health plans used the results to improve quality within their plans, but the results were also used to market health plans to employers. Of course, the creators of the plans wanted the plans to perform well and went to great lengths to train auditors and ensure data collection was accurate. Unfortunately, measuring the performance of individual physicians was not part of this project. I believe a tool measuring physician performance should be developed for consumers to use. Nurses receive annual performance reviews in any employment setting. Who evaluates physicians?

I am no longer auditing but remain very much interested in the discussions about the future of health care in America. The United States continues to spend considerably more on health care than any other country yet does not have a higher life expectancy. We are not even in the list of the top ten countries in this category. Interestingly, the life expectancy of the citizens of Canada and the United Kingdom are greater than the United States—and those two countries have socialized medicine! If only the media would repeat this to the American public as often as they repeat the same tired celebrity stories.

My suggestions to reduce health care costs start with redirecting the mindset of America to once again focus on the family doctor model instead of emphasizing specialists. We could expand training and improve compensation for family practitioners. Years ago, I read that most doctor visits were for garden variety conditions, ailments like sore throats, lumps, bumps, skin problems, stomach distress. Specialists were consulted for complicated cases or when treatments failed. Today, referrals are so frequent it appears some primary care providers have become merely go-betweens. The concept of "tincture of time"— give the body a little time to resolve the problem before ordering expensive tests—has evaporated.

Once a patient goes to a specialist that patient will most assuredly receive "specialized" testing with the latest diagnostic tools. An ER physician I worked with years ago shared this insight: "Today's diagnostic tools are so sophisticated that it's impossible not to find something wrong with everyone." And what's troubling is that after people see a specialist, they are often told to return for routine follow-up *for years*. Why can't the family doctor take over routine monitoring after a successful specialist consult and intervention? The system cannot sustain the cost of specialist visits to dispense "blessings" only. A family member, who is a nurse practitioner, told me she can't understand why so many healthy people are making annual visits to so many "ologists." To further argue my point about referrals, I'm sharing some personal experiences here. My healthy adult son was sent to an ear, nose, and, throat specialist by his primary care physician to have earwax removed. Earwax was the only finding at the visit to the specialist. I shared the story at work. A coworker, a former pediatric nurse, informed me the nurses routinely removed earwax using irrigation at the office where she used to work. I told my son to find a new doctor.

My sister was sent to a GI specialist after seeing her doctor for acid indigestion. Her primary care physician never asked if certain foods exacerbated her symptoms or told her to stop eating a few hours before bedtime. The GI specialist never discussed diet or times of eating in association with bedtime either. Instead, my sister immediately had an endoscopy and was told she had some mild irritation—and then she was dismissed with an expensive prescription, like probably untold thousands of other patients. She has since converted her prescription to TUMS, which is available over-the-counter, because of her copays. She also figured out that what and when she ate really did make a difference.

The number of prescriptions the average American fills today is mind-boggling. Has the increase been associated with an increase in life expectancy or quality of life? Has direct marketing to the public by the pharmaceutical companies contributed to an increase in prescriptions? *Has anyone ever looked at this issue?*

I think it could be very beneficial for the National Institutes of Health, along with a coalition of companies from the insurance industry, to set up a task force, totally independent of the pharmaceutical industry, to study annual pharmaceutical use. The coalition could review the top ten prescribed medications and the top ten cost generators and make recommendations on the indications for the use of each and possible alternatives. Most importantly, the coalition should release the findings to the public instead of burying the results in medical journals.

I've observed that many people are unaware of the side effects of medications. Pharmacies provide a printout when we pick up prescriptions, but it is usually so long that most people don't bother to read it. It is troubling to me that the real picture of the incidence of side effects associated with any given drug may not be accurate, because this metric is dependent on reporting at the level of individual physicians' offices.

The amount and extent of documentation required by nurses in hospitals and home health seems excessive; reduces productivity, and should be addressed. A neighbor who was an experienced home health nurse informed me the admission paperwork was fifteen pages and took the average nurse approximately an hour to complete. He said he could complete the assessment with a few simple requests to the patient and document his findings in a few sentences. He would ask the date, the name of the president and then tell them to take their shoes off and walk across the room. He would then ask them to put their shoes back on. This showed hearing, vision, cognitive function and mobility. Pretty impressive.

Hospital nurse friends tell me there is too much redundancy in required documentation. Even if a physician has just visited and documented on a patient, nurses are required to fill out total body assessment check sheets at the start of every shift instead of charting just pertinent findings. Before she died, my mother-in-law said to me, "Nurses don't seem to take care of patients anymore, they take care of machines." Sometimes it seems the number one machine nurses care for is called a COW—a computer on wheels (the computer sits on a cart with wheels) which is what nurses use to do their documentation.

A significant number of questionable people seem to be on disability today. They include a fifty-year-old woman who rides her bike around the neighborhood daily and can make herself into a pretzel at yoga class. She seems to have conquered her disabling back problem but apparently has never been reevaluated. Another neighbor retired early on disability after shoulder surgery for a problem caused by a repetitive factory job. I wondered how a disabled man could move the furniture out of his home and load it onto a POD. The neighbors saw him do this as he prepared to move out of state to retire in the sunshine. A nurse friend of mine suggested that it should be easy to get disability but harder than hell to stay on it.

Once I visited a man on Medicaid at his home. It was situated in a neighborhood of homes in the $300,000 price range. A couple of expensive cars sat in the driveway. His wife answered the door wearing designer clothes and a huge diamond. The home was tastefully furnished. In addition to enjoying his palatial home the man belonged to a gym, yet he claimed no income. I reported my findings to the state but found they don't have the resources to investigate. This needs to change.

The insurance companies should reduce their product lines and simplify the rules. I think it is unacceptable for consumers to pay enormous monthly premiums, receive a book detailing the plan, and then find they missed some "fine print" about coverage or get inaccurate information from customer service. I was self-employed at my last job, and before I became eligible for Medicare I bought a policy under the Affordable Care Act. I was turned away at several doctor's offices because they didn't take my insurance, a bit of a rude awakening. However, I fully realize that many people employed on company insurance plans also have limited choices. Some companies offer only a single plan, an HMO, to keep costs down. I haven't seen this information tracked, trended, or publicized in the news.

I firmly believe the "positives" of a one-payer system far out-weighs the negatives. Too many people were denied care in the past because of preexisting conditions, and they suffered dire financial hardship or inadequate care as a result. I have no problem with the concept that everyone should pay into the system. Hospitals will always raise their rates to compensate for the care provided to the uninsured, which is part of the reason insurance premiums increase. States require people to purchase auto insurance, so why not require health insurance or a mandate that everyone should contribute something to the health care pot if they choose not to be insured? I wonder where we are on the issue of investigating fraud in the medical equipment industry. TV news shows have profiled fraudulent companies consisting only of "shell" storefronts that have bilked Medicare for millions. I would like to know what anti-fraud measures are in place.

While I believe most physicians are competent and decent, they need to do a better job of weeding out those who are not. There is a National Practitioners Data Bank but I am uncertain how the information is used by hospitals or if it is available to the general public. We have the capability to compare outcomes for hospital stays by collecting readmission rates, death rates, and surgical complication rates, such as the incidence of perforations after an endoscopy or the incidence of a stroke after carotid surgery. I am not aware if any of this information is readily available to the pub-lic either, but it should be.

Nurses should sit on all hospital quality committees. At least one of these nurse representatives should be a "hands on" nurse rather than an administrative nurse. I often wonder if there are nurses at congressional health policy meetings; we could offer a wealth of insight.

Nursing compensation may never compete with compensation in the business world, but I was rewarded in a better way: being able to enjoy the satisfaction of meeting and helping so many incredible people. They shared their life stories and showed me courage and dignity, and they taught me patience. Bringing back someone from the brink of catastrophe—and sometimes the brink of death—is a high I don't think many people experience in their jobs. I am proud to be a nurse.